The Journal of Best Practices

*A Memoir
of Marriage,
Asperger Syndrome, and
One Man's Quest
to Be a Better Husband*

David Finch

Scribner

New York   London   Toronto   Sydney   New Delhi

SCRIBNER
A Division of Simon & Schuster, Inc.
1230 Avenue of the Americas
New York, NY 10020

Author's Note: This is a memoir. I have been faithful to my recollections. Certain events and dialogue have been adapted to suit the narrative. The names and identifying characteristics of some individuals have been changed.

First Scribner trade paperback edition October 2012

SCRIBNER and design are registered trademarks of The Gale Group, Inc., used under license by Simon & Schuster, Inc., the publisher of this work.

For information about special discounts for bulk purchases, please contact Simon & Schuster Special Sales at 1-866-506-1949 or business@simonandschuster.com.

The Simon & Schuster Speakers Bureau can bring authors to your live event. For more information or to book an event contact the Simon & Schuster Speakers Bureau at 1-866-248-3049 or visit our website at www.simonspeakers.com.

Designed by Carla Jayne Jones

Manufactured in the United States of America

10 9 8 7 6 5 4 3 2 1

Library of Congress Control Number: 2011013986

ISBN 978-1-4391-8971-9
ISBN 978-1-4391-8974-0 (pbk)
ISBN 978-1-4391-8975-7 (ebook)

To Kristen, Emily, and Parker

"The only thing to know is how to use your neuroses."

—*Arthur Adamov*

Contents

Introduction

Do all that you can
to be worthy of her love.

I was thirty years old and had been married five years when I learned that I have Asperger syndrome, a relatively mild form of autism. My wife, Kristen, a speech therapist and autism expert, brought it to my attention one evening after harboring suspicions for years.

Receiving such a diagnosis as an adult might seem shocking and unsettling. It wasn't. Eye-opening, yes. Life-changing, yes. But not distressing in the least. Strangely, it was rather empowering to discover that I had this particular condition. In fact, the diagnosis ultimately changed my life for the better.

I received the news the day before my niece was born. I remember this not because I'm a wonderful uncle but because she was born on March 14, 2008, which is well-known among my fellow nerds in the math and science communities as "Pi Day" because pi, the ratio of a circle's circumference to its diameter, is equal to 3.14. Also 3 + 14 + 2 + 0 + 8 totals 27, which is divisible by 3, and I love numbers that are divisible by 3, particularly numbers whose digits sum to 27, of which

3 is the cube root. (Are you starting to see why Kristen had her suspicions?)

The day had been chaotic but really nothing out of the ordinary for two young working parents. Kristen was in the kitchen, trying to put it back in some kind of order, and I was upstairs saying good night to our kids. After walking with our ten-month-old son, Parker, in little circles around his dark room and whispering the lyrics of an Eric Clapton song until he fell asleep, I cuddled with our daughter, Emily, until her restless two-year-old squirming subsided and her breathing slowed and deepened. I crept out, whispering "I love you," the words all but dissolving into the whir of her electric fan.

As I descended into the warm amber glow that bathed the first floor of our house, I could hear the hum of the dishwasher in the kitchen and the soft clunk of toys being put away in the playroom. Something was up; the house was never so tranquil right after the kids went to bed. Usually, the television was on, the kitchen was a disaster, and books and toys were scattered everywhere. I expected to find Kristen in her usual spot: sitting on the couch among stacks of paper and thick binders, her laptop resting on her legs as she feverishly prepared for the next day's work. But everything was different that night.

In the kitchen, my dinner was cooling on the clean counter, and I felt an unusual sense of peace as I prepared for my evening routine. At eight thirty each night, after the kids have been put to bed, I circle the first floor, counterclockwise, starting in the kitchen, where I check to see if the patio door is locked. Then it's back to the kitchen, where I usually wander around in circles until Kristen asks me what I'm doing.

But that night, before I began, Kristen approached me by the refrigerator in her pajamas and wrapped me in a tight hug.

"Oh," I said, surprised. "Hello there." I couldn't remember the last time she had given me a hug for no particular reason. I hesitated for a moment, trying to play it cool, then squeezed her close.

"Hi," she said into my chest. Her blond hair darkened to a shade of honey and shimmered lightly in the dimness. "Do you want some pizza?" she asked.

"Yeah, thanks for making it."

"Sure," she said. "When you're ready, why don't you bring it down to the basement?" Without letting go, she looked up at me and smiled. "There's something I want to show you."

"Okay, I'll be right down."

Understanding the importance of my routines, she playfully patted my butt and headed down to her office in the basement. Stunned by this rare and remarkable display of affection, I completed my rounds. I proceeded through the dining room and living room, then it was on to the foyer, where I always take a few moments to stare out the front window, visually lining up the neighbors' rooftops (the alignment is the same every time, which is so gratifying it makes my shoulders relax, and for a moment my head is clear, my thoughts organized). As usual, I took note of which lights were on. I don't normally shut them off, I just like to check in and see how they're doing. *Dining room light on, piano lamp not on, foyer not on, hallway on, kitchen off (that's kind of rare . . . how 'bout it, kitchen?), oven hood on.* I grabbed my pizza from the counter, swiped a Pepsi from the fridge, and made my way down the loud, clunky steps to Kristen's office in our basement, where she was sitting in front of her computer. She turned and beamed at me.

"Sit here," she said, pointing to the empty chair beside her. I had no idea what was going on, but there was pizza involved, and for the first time in weeks, I'd made her smile. *Whatever it is, I'm in.*

"Ready to get down to business?" she asked in a tone that seemed to suggest that I was.

I laughed. "Wet's get down to bwass tacks!"

"Huh?" She looked thoroughly confused.

"It's from *Blazing Saddles*. I'm ready."

Embarrassed and disappointed that my movie reference tanked,

I shoved my hands under my legs and swiveled back and forth in my chair.

"All right," she said. "I'm going to ask you a list of questions, and you just have to answer honestly." She must have realized that she was setting herself up by telling me to answer honestly. I tend to be verbose when people ask me to talk about myself; some would even say exhausting. I have no filter to limit my discourse to relevant things, and that puts people off. When I am invited to speak about myself, often what comes forth is the verbal equivalent of a volcanic eruption, spewing molten mind magma in every direction.

"I mean, you don't have to deliberate each question," she said, backpedaling. "I don't need big, long answers, just honest ones."

"Got it."

She began: "Do you tend to get so absorbed by your special interests that you forget or ignore everything else? Just answer yes, no, or sometimes."

"Special interests?"

"You know," she said, "things like practicing your saxophone for four hours a day, or when you wrote scenes at the Second City and I hardly ever saw you . . ."

"Oh, well, sure," I said. We both laughed. "I mean, doesn't everybody get into stuff?"

"No," she replied, marking down my answer. "Many people can do something they enjoy and not let it consume their whole life so they forget to pay bills, or put on shoes, or check in on their family from time to time."

"Well. That's their problem if they don't have the intellectual capacity to engage constructively with an activity."

"Next one: Is your sense of humor different from the mainstream or considered odd?"

I reflected back on the moment thirty seconds earlier, when I had cracked myself up by throwing my head back and bellowing what would be for most people a forgettable line from a Mel Brooks movie. Then I recalled going to a Victoria's Secret store fifteen years earlier with my friend Greg and convincing the salesclerk that my girlfriend was shaped exactly like me, just so that I could quickly try on some lingerie against store policy (apparently) and give Greg a good laugh. That joke had been a success. But then I remembered the time in junior high when I glued a rubber chicken head to a T-shirt and wrote LET'S GET SERIOUS across the chest in permanent marker, only to be told at school that I'd have to wear something more appropriate. That time nobody had laughed. Finally, I recalled going to dinner with a customer a year earlier and taking a series of dirty jokes so far that he abruptly stopped laughing and asked what was wrong with me.

"Put me down for a yes," I concluded.

"Do you often talk about your special interests whether others seem interested or not?" she asked. Her smile was answer enough, and I assumed that, like me, she was thinking of all the times in which I'd waxed lyrical about having perfected the art of using public toilets.

"Yes." *What else is there to talk about?*

On and on it went, for over 150 questions.

"Do you take an interest in, and remember, details that others do not seem to notice? Do you notice patterns in things all the time? Do you need periods of contemplation?" All emphatically answered yes, with a follow-up, "This is fun!"

"Do you tend to get so stuck on details that you miss the overall picture? Do you get very tired after socializing and need to regenerate alone? Do people comment on your unusual mannerisms and habits?" *Absolutely!*

I found the questions rather amusing until we came to a section so personally revealing that it pulled the air from my lungs and made me forget how to blink.

"Does it feel vitally important to be left undisturbed when focusing on your special interests?" she asked. "*Vitally* is the key here."

"Yes. You know how—"

"I know," Kristen said, interrupting. "Before doing something or going somewhere, do you need to have a picture in your mind of what's going to happen so as to be able to prepare yourself mentally first?"

This question seems rather insightful. "O-oh my God," I stammered. "Yeah, that's totally me."

"Do you prefer to wear the same clothes and eat the same food every day? Do you become intensely frustrated if an activity that is important to you gets interrupted? Do you have strong attachments to certain favorite objects?"

"Those are all yes."

"I know. Do you have certain routines which you need to follow? Do you get frustrated if you can't sit on your favorite seat?"

"I literally have ended friendships over the seat thing. In high school—"

"Do you feel tortured by clothes tags, clothes that are too tight or are made in the 'wrong' material? Do you tend to shut down or have a meltdown when stressed or overwhelmed?"

All yes. But I was too stunned to answer aloud.

"How about, do people think you are aloof and distant? Do you often feel out of sync with others? In conversations, do you need extra time to carefully think out your reply, so that there may be a pause before you answer? Have you had the feeling of playing a game, pretending to be like people around you?"

I had chills. Actually, my skin was on fire. Actually, it was both.

"What is this?" I asked.

"Just keep answering honestly." Kristen patted my leg reassuringly. "You'll find out when we're done."

One by one, the questions described everything I already knew about myself—everything that I had always felt made me unique, beautiful, yet removed from other people. Folding my arms tight, I began to cry, which surprised both of us.

Kristen asked if I was all right, and I said that I was, so we continued. Another batch of questions brought back the laughter. In fact, most of the questions from that point forward were rather potent, evoking one strong emotion or another, though there were a few that seemed odd and out of place, such as "Do you sometimes have an urge to jump over things?" and "Have you been fascinated by making traps?" (Admittedly, it sucked a little to hear myself answering yes to both of those.)

We finished the quiz, and Kristen took a moment to gaze at me before asking, "What do you think?"

"I think that was a very telling list of questions," I said. "Did you write those?"

She explained that she had stumbled upon the questionnaire while searching online for Asperger's evaluation resources, though, notably, she offered little explanation as to *why* she had been looking for those resources. I had to assume that it wasn't strictly for her job.

I felt like I was free-falling. "Okay," I said.

"Ready to find out what it says?"

"Sure," I said, though I was anything but.

Kristen clicked the mouse and my score flashed onto the screen: 155 out of a possible 200.

"One fifty-five?" I asked. "What is that? Is that a lot?"

"That's a whole lotta Asperger's," she said, nodding.

"Are you serious?"

"That's what it says."

"I have Asperger's? I have autism?! I mean . . . holy shit! Right?"

"Dave, you don't have autism. You don't even officially have an Asperger's diagnosis. This is just a self-quiz and I'm not a doctor, but I think you may have Asperger syndrome. That's why I wanted you to take this quiz. Based on your score, you'd probably receive the diagnosis if a doctor gave you a formal evaluation."

I repeated myself: "Holy shit!"

At that point, all I knew about Asperger syndrome was what I'd heard from Kristen over the years. I understood that it was an autism spectrum condition and that those with Asperger's had a difficult time engaging with others socially. I knew a few people with Asperger syndrome—diagnosed children and adults—and they seemed to function at different levels; some had obvious telltale behaviors while others could have been written off as shy or odd. I also understood that it could easily be misdiagnosed.

Wanting to know if the online quiz was a reliable weather vane, I asked Kristen—who is perhaps the most un-Asperger's person that I know—to evaluate herself. She agreed, and scored an eight.

A few minutes passed as I sat on my hands, rocking back and forth, trying to process what I had just learned. Kristen sat patiently, keeping her eyes trained on me, waiting for my reaction. I was not upset. I was not conflicted. The knowledge felt amazing. It was cathartic. And it made perfect sense. *Of course!* Here were answers, handed to me so easily, to almost every difficult question I'd had since childhood: Why is it so hard for me to engage with people? Why do I seem to perceive and process things so differently from everyone else? Why do the sounds and phrases that play in a continuous loop in my head seem louder and command more attention than the actual world around me? In other words, why am I different? *Oh my God, I have Asperger's!*

While someone else might question why his wife would sit him down and informally evaluate him for Asperger syndrome—in her pajamas, no less—at no point during that evening in Kristen's office did I wonder about it. For one thing, there are certain orders and tasks that I simply don't dispute; I just follow commands and generally do whatever people tell me to. But there's no particular consistency to this, which is strange. Frequent requests from Kristen such as "Please remember to run the dishwasher tonight" don't have much of an effect. But if I walked into a grocery store and someone grabbed my elbow and asked me to put on a hot dog costume, two minutes later I'd be standing there, a six-foot wiener in a neoprene bun, wondering how long I was supposed to keep it on.

What I found most remarkable about that evening—besides the part where I found out that I have Asperger syndrome—was that Kristen and I had shared some good hours together for the first time in months. There was laughter and insight and deep discussion. There was warmth and affection and unmistakable love—I could see it in her eyes, feel it in our closeness. Though we had been married only five years, such moments had become painfully rare. We both knew that our marriage had fallen apart, that our mutual feelings of helplessness and disappointment had pushed aside the fun and happiness we once shared, and more than once we found ourselves wondering if a separation was the only way out. Of course it wasn't gloom and doom all the time, but I couldn't deny the fact that we were estranged. That was not something we had ever envisioned happening to our relationship.

But once I learned that I have Asperger syndrome, the fact that we'd had these serious marital problems seemed less surprising. Asperger syndrome can manifest itself in behaviors that are inherently relationship defeating. It's tricky being married to me, though neither Kristen nor I could have predicted that. To the casual neurotypical observer (*neurotypical* refers to people with typically functioning brains, i.e., people without autism), I may seem relatively normal. Cognitive resources and language skills often develop normally in people with Asperger syndrome, which means that in many situations I could probably pass myself off as neurotypical, were it not for four distinguishing characteristics of my disorder: persistent, intense preoccupations; unusual rituals and behaviors; impaired social-reasoning abilities; and clinical-strength egocentricity. All of which I have to an almost comically high degree. But I also have the ability to mask these effects under the right circumstances, like when I want someone to hire me or fall in love with me.

Looking back, I suppose a diagnosis was inevitable. A casual girl-friend might have dismissed my compulsion to arrange balls of shred-ded napkin into symmetrical shapes as being idiosyncratic or even artistic. But Kristen had been living with me—observing me for years in my natural habitat—and had become increasingly skilled in assessing autism spectrum conditions in her job as a speech therapist. While it is technically inaccurate to say that she *diagnosed* me (that wouldn't have been possible or ethical, as she's not a doctor), as far as I was concerned, I *had* received a diagnosis that evening. I went to bed 100 percent con-vinced that I had Asperger syndrome. I later received a formal Asperger's diagnosis from a doctor, but that exercise hardly seemed necessary. Given my behaviors, it would have been just as easy to diagnose a nosebleed.

One of my most obvious symptoms is the way I handle myself in unexpected social interactions. Especially conversations, which involve many subtle rules. My problem is that I can't seem to learn and apply the rules properly, though not for lack of trying. One is simply supposed to know the right way to respond to people or initiate conversations, but my attempts rarely pass muster. And due to my intense preoccupations with certain things, I have a tendency to discuss very strange topics at length, oblivious to the listener's level of interest. A typical conversation might go something like this:

"How 'bout those Bears, Dave?" a colleague will ask.

"I don't really follow sports, so I decline to form an opinion other than that I like their uniforms. It's funny you mention bears because last night I was reading about grizzly bears, which are my favorite kind of bear, and I learned something rather unsettling about their mating habits."

"Never mind."

My responses confound people, I'm garrulous about all the wrong things, my speech is awkward, and then there's also my not-at-all-charming delay in processing, which makes for disjointed conversation and missed social cues. Conversations either persist much longer than either party would like them to ("And here's *another* thing that fascinates me about sewing machines . . ."), or they end too quickly ("You did hear correctly, we had a baby yesterday and it wasn't without its complications. See you later"). Even if I manage to deliver my point, it's usually somewhat irrelevant. ("So I guess what I'm trying to say about the Civil War is, how about the beards on those soldiers, huh? Where's everybody going?")

Over the years, I have learned some ways to compensate. When I know ahead of time who I'll encounter in a particular situation, I can prepare. I have a strong tendency to assume characters—versions of myself that are optimized for the social environment at hand. Conversations must be scripted, facial expressions rehearsed, personalities summoned. This strategy has enabled me to succeed at work and in school and to do well enough socially. If I'm with conservative work colleagues, I'm reserved and willing to discuss Christianity and handgun rights. Neighbors enjoy a lawn-care enthusiast and classic-rock fan when I arrive at the block party, and Kristen's relatives are always excited to see the gregarious, supportive man who values a respectful handshake. Whatever the occasion, and whichever corresponding persona I choose to wear for it, pulling off a successful social exchange is a lot of work. It's exhausting. I don't know how neurotypicals do it, let alone how they look forward to it.

Under the right conditions, I do enjoy going out with friends. We've already established common ground and I know what they expect from me. I get high from making people laugh, from performing. Goofing around with my buddies is still tremendously hard work requiring much preparation, but at least there's a payoff: laughter. When I am on, and I'm with the right people, I am killing and full of deranged brilliance (I like to think). A pita may be swiped from someone's plate and used as a potty-mouthed talking vagina, or I may demonstrate what I believe would be a controversial but effective new wiping technique for the bathroom. They laugh, go home, and wake up the next morning with real-world problems on their minds. I go home to review my performance. *Was the talking pita vagina too potty-mouthed? Did the elderly couple a few tables over think I was boorish? How might I incorporate beating off into the bit about folk musicians?* My head spins as it hits the pillow.

The social aspect, however, is only one piece of the Asperger's puzzle. Sensory issues present another problem for me. As humans, we learn about our world through sensory stimulation. But for me, certain sensations become so overwhelming that I lose control of myself. While most people can go about their business oblivious to their partially untucked shirts and itchy sweater collars, I suffer major emotional tailspins over something as supposedly minor as pilly jean pockets. On many occasions, I've had to excuse myself from meetings at work to duck into the men's room, take off my clothes, and completely redress myself because my underwear has bunched up, or my socks have twisted around my shins, or, heaven forbid, my shirt has static buildup. My solution is to buy several identical garments that feel all right against my skin, then wear them over and over until they fall apart. Take away the black jacket (those sleeves would drive me mental), and I'm like the Michael Kors of the Asperger's community.

Of course, sensory issues and clumsy social exchanges don't ruin marriages. What brought my marriage to its knees were my God-given egocentricity and inability to cope with situations and circumstances beyond my control. Put the two qualities together, and you're left with something that looks like a combination of pathological closed-mindedness and an obsessive-compulsive disorder. OCD might not take down a marriage, but I'm certain that pathological closed-mindedness isn't one of the top qualities a person would look for in a spouse.

Everybody likes to have things in order, and everybody likes things to go according to plan. But because of the way my brain developed, I *need* things to be in order, and I *need* things to go as planned. If they don't, I come unglued. If left unchecked, my reactions resemble the tantrums my two-year-old would throw whenever someone would disturb his meticulous line of toy train cars. My inability to cope partially explains my horrible flash temper. If the grocery store is out of my preferred hamburger buns, for example, three hours later it will result in a nuclear reaction of cynicism and anger. The disruption of my routine is so upsetting that I can't—not won't, *can't*—contain myself, and everyone around me sees the unpleasant effects. I've been told a million times to "get over it," but I can't. My brain won't let me. Just as I can't seem to prevent the regrettable outbursts that usually follow.

My preoccupations or obsessions often play a big part in this. To avoid meltdowns, I indulge certain obsessions, often at the expense of being on time for things. I *must* eat eggs and cereal for breakfast, for example. If we are out of cereal, then I will go to the grocery store and buy some, even if people are waiting for me at work. I may arrive at the office a couple hours late, but I'm satisfied and ready to focus on my assignments.

Fortunately, I have an assortment of routines that are very calming when properly executed. If my intense preoccupations resemble Obsession, then my calming rituals would be like Obsession's diaper-wearing pet monkey, Compulsion. I spend my day lining certain items up just so, tapping or lightly touching objects in a particular way, and gazing at my own penmanship. The compulsive behaviors are really quite small and limited, and with the exception of my nightly circling the house, having to correctly perform a mental ritual before exiting certain rooms, flicking light switches on and off, and repeatedly opening and closing doors, they're really not all that intrusive. They tend to become more pronounced when I'm anxious about something, but all things considered, I've got it easy.

Kristen, on the other hand, doesn't have it so easy. She's married to all of this. Her frustration is inevitable, no matter how much she loves me. But that's how it goes, especially in neurologically mixed marriages such as mine. Were I just another one of the kids she works with, Kristen wouldn't be frustrated by me. But I'm her husband.

Kristen and I had been friends since high school, had fallen in love after college, and had gotten married shortly thereafter. During the years we dated, I was on my best behavior. *Don't talk about semiconductors all night,* I'd remind myself. *Remember to keep the conversation moving and focused on things she likes, such as Vince Vaughn and clothes. If she doesn't feel like eating hamburgers for dinner, just be okay with it and don't flip out.*

When I slipped, she seemed to find my eccentricity endearing. I remember her laughter upon discovering dozens of pictures I had taken of myself to see what I might look like to other people at any given moment: me watching TV; me about to sneeze; me on the toilet, looking pensive.

She loved the story of how I took an emergency leave from work to boil my glasses after they had fallen from my shirt pocket in a men's room stall. She found it pitifully charming when I would stand alone at parties, kind of dancing, or follow her from room to room, unable to engage with anyone else.

It was all so charming until we got married and there was nowhere for Hyde to hide. I became incapable of concealing the truly damaging behaviors I'd managed to stave off for so long—selfishness, meltdowns, emotional detachment. She never saw it coming. With people I like and for short periods of time, I've always been able to sustain a wonderful version of myself. With enough effort, I can even pull off enchanting. (Prince Charming is one of my most highly developed characters.) This was how I won Kristen over when we began dating. Because I was able to keep up appearances for a long while, it came as a major surprise to both of us when, a few months into our marriage, she started seeing through the ever-widening cracks in the facade I'd created, revealing the person I'd been since childhood, someone who wasn't programmed to be an ideal, supportive partner.

I never meant to pull a fast one or to deceive Kristen in any way. I was profoundly in love with her. Like anyone, I wanted to put my best self out there, and thanks to the intoxicating effects of new love, I genuinely believed that I would forever be that best version of myself. But not long after we were married, my handful of endearing quirks began to multiply, making me, as a husband, exponentially more annoying and harder to deal with. Quirks are like sneezes or energetic puppies— one or two aren't so bad, but try dealing with ten thousand of them. Eventually, Kristen's life became flooded with my neuroses, and she found herself wondering who in the hell she'd married.

She was, for example, understanding when I first insisted that all groceries be purchased from the Jewel-Osco grocery store, but when I started demanding they be purchased from the Jewel-Osco grocery store two towns over, rather than from the one right by our house, she protested. "'Because that one has a better vibe' is not reason enough," she said, but I had no other way to explain why the routine of going to that store was so critical. It just was.

When we were stuck in a traffic jam following a multiple-vehicle pileup, she listened for an hour as I speculated on the questionable driving habits of the victims before turning up the volume on the radio and saying to me, "People are probably dead. Can you please try and have an ounce of compassion?"

And annoyed by my constant questioning about how long the Thanksgiving feast at Aunt Deb's might last she snapped, "Why does it matter how long the dinner will be? I have no clue. None. Get over it."

Ashamed by my apparent insanity, by a personality I couldn't seem to control, I slowly withdrew from Kristen over the first few years of our marriage. Confused and disappointed, she allowed herself to do the same. I resigned myself to the belief that we were fundamentally incompatible and that this was to blame for our resentment toward each other, the terrible distance between us, the way she was cold to me but would spring to life around everyone else. For years we just didn't know how to fix it. This wasn't the life I had imagined living, and so I felt all along that our marriage had failed me. It had never occurred to me to step back and look at the situation differently—to concede that perhaps our marriage had failed because I had failed our marriage.

My diagnosis changed everything for us. The impact of the knowledge was deep and immediate. "This explains so much," we kept saying. Of course, when I said it, the implication was that the diagnosis explained so much about me and my life. Now, looking back, I understand that when Kristen said it she had meant "This explains so much about *us*." (How's that for egocentricity?) The instant my score was calculated my alienating, baffling behaviors were transformed into well-documented symptoms of a known disorder—they no longer seemed malicious and unexplainable. Kristen understood that the damaging behaviors were not my fault, exactly, and was able to see me in a new light. Her resentment vanished; I was forgiven.

Kristen went to bed that evening feeling better than she had in years, she told me. After she went upstairs I stayed in her office, in front of her computer. I decided to research autism spectrum conditions, knowing that I would not be able to shut off my brain and go to sleep that night. Every website I visited, every personal account I read, every clinical paper I skimmed was another helpful resource, more good news for me.

At some point, in the hours that I spent absorbed in research and raw self-discovery, something occurred to me: *I process things differently from Kristen, I'm as socially functional as a tuba, I don't look beyond my own needs and my own interests, I haven't been talking to her, and I behave very strangely. No wonder our marriage sucks right now. I think this Asperger syndrome may just be what's destroying our marriage!* I know, I know—great detective work. But with that discovery, I felt as though I'd been reborn. The reason we struggled for so long to find solutions to the problems in our marriage was that we hadn't understood their causes. Identifying the source and knowing that it affected millions of other people made for a very short leap to the conclusion that I could finally do something about it. *We're screwed* suddenly became *We're saved!*

It's amazing how swiftly a spot diagnosis can catalyze change. As a teenager, I was diagnosed with attention deficit disorder (ADD)—first unofficially, by my mom, and then officially by a doctor. I've been taking Ritalin or something like it ever since, and it works. The medication helps me to process information, focus my thoughts, and keep myself organized at a functional level that I can't achieve on my own. But there is no silver bullet that will eliminate all the difficulties that come with Asperger's. If there had been a single pill that would help me to put the needs of others before my own, to rid my life of meltdowns and control issues, and to help me to be a highly sociable person, then I would have been mighty tempted to take it, if only to stop annoying everyone around me. But I couldn't take a pill that would accomplish all of that—it doesn't exist—so I decided to take initiative.

Armed with knowledge and new self-awareness, I could start looking every day for ways to manage the behaviors that had been wreaking havoc on our marriage. *Address the causes and the symptoms will vanish.* I wasn't interested in a complete personality overhaul; I just wanted to become more in control of myself.

"I think I can fix our marriage," I said to Kristen the following morning. "I'm basically the one who destroyed it, and now that I know what my behaviors are doing to us, I can start working on ways to improve myself."

"Dave, that's awesome, but it's not all because of you," she said. "You didn't destroy our marriage, and I hope you know that. I'd say there's a lot that we both need to work on in our relationship, and we can do it together."

"Sounds good to me." I had no idea what she intended to sort out from her side; I was so focused on myself that I didn't even bother to ask.

We also agreed that there was a lot about me that we hoped would never change. The harmless little quirks that, in Kristen's words, "made me Dave": achieving perfectly consistent spacing between all ten fingers, getting carried away with an internal recitation of a phrase to the point where it blurts from my lips ("Heyoooo!"), repeatedly snapping pictures of myself. These were the things we wanted to keep. However, doing those things while she and the kids wait outside in the car, late for our son's baptism, well, that's exactly the sort of thing I was hoping to overcome.

My hope was that by transforming myself, I would bring about some transformation in our marriage. Transforming myself would mean changing my behaviors, and I knew it wouldn't be simple or easy. If it were, I probably would have done it long ago.

Most people intuitively know how to function and interact with people—they don't need to learn it by rote. I do. I was certain that with enough discipline and hard work I could learn to improve my behaviors and become more adaptable. While my brain is not wired for social intuition, I was factory-programmed to observe, analyze, and mimic the world around me. I had managed to go through school, get a good job, make friends, and marry—years of observation, processing, and trial and error had gotten me this far. And my obsessive tendencies mean that when I want to accomplish something I attack it with zeal. With my marriage in dire straits, I decided that even if I needed to make flash cards about certain behaviors and staple them to my face to make them become second nature, I was willing to do it.

Kristen didn't know it, but that was what her life was about to become—her husband, with the best of intentions, stapling flash cards to his face. Okay, not to his face. And there were no staples involved. But flash cards? Definitely. Many people leave reminder notes for themselves: *Pick up milk and shampoo*, or *Dinner with the Hargroves at 6:00*. My notes read: *Respect the needs of others*, and *Do not laugh during visitation tonight*, and *Do not EVER suggest that Kristen doesn't seem to enjoy spending time with our kids*.

Opportunity for change was everywhere, I noticed. When I thought of something I wanted to address, or when I learned something in an argument with Kristen, I would write it down. *Don't change the radio station when she's singing along. When she's on the phone, don't force yourself into the conversation. Don't sneak up on her.* I wrote these little gems everywhere: on loose-leaf paper, in my notebooks and journals, on my computer and phone. One particularly intense series of realizations, which ultimately led to remarkable breakthroughs in our relationship, was recorded on an envelope that I kept in the pocket of my car door.

In order to keep up with the rapid pace of inspiration, I started keeping a journal—the Journal of Best Practices. This wasn't some huge, leather-bound diary that I kept under my pillow, as one might expect. That wouldn't have been practical, since there was no telling where I'd be when my feverish rumination would cough up a new best practice. Rather, the Journal of Best Practices was my collection of notes. I could have called it my Nightstand Drawer of Best Practices, since that's where most of the scraps of paper, envelopes, and actual journals ended up—but what kind of wacko keeps a Nightstand Drawer of Best Practices?

Collectively, the entries in my Journal of Best Practices would become my guiding principles. Some of them would stick. Others would not. Some would be laughably obvious (*Don't hog all the crab rangoon*), and certain others would be revealed only after many painful scenes. Even so, the hardest work would lie not in formulating the Best Practices but in implementing them. But with our happiness at stake, that's what I'd learn to do.

Chapter 1

Be her friend, first and always.

When people who know me first meet Kristen, I've learned not to be surprised when they pull me aside later and ask, "How is it that you wound up with someone like her?"

The question may be valid, but validity doesn't relieve the sting of indictment. It's a question that implies two things. Namely, that I am the walking manifestation of circus music, and while I may be qualified to do certain things, landing a good-looking, interesting woman wouldn't be one of them. I find it especially annoying when people say this in front of Kristen. Even if it's meant as a joke, have some class. Normally, I laugh and make little self-effacing jokes, but Kristen usually replies, "There's just something about him, I guess," and beams at me as brightly as she can.

Her smiling but firm reply always neatly puts the person in their place. "We're done taking shots at my husband now," it says. I like it because I know what she means when she says it. I understand why we're together. I know what she sees in me, most days. So when Kristen isn't there to defend me, I find that it's best to explain it simply: "We've been friends since high school, and at some point, I won her over."

What better way to say it? Our friendship has always served as a reminder of how happy we can be together, a mark on our compass even in the darkest of moments when we lost sight of what our marriage was supposed to have been.

As if having Asperger syndrome didn't make me cool enough, in high school, I chose—to the exclusion of playing sports, taking drugs, or beating up nerds—to get involved in all things music. I wasn't just in the band, I had to be in four school bands: concert, wind, jazz, and (coolest of all) marching. I wasn't just in the choir, I had to sing in two select choirs: a cappella choir and the snazzy jazz vocal ensemble, MACH-1: Music At Contemporary Heights . . . One. I went for singing and dancing roles in the musical productions *Hello, Dolly!, Annie, Brigadoon,* and *Little Shop of Horrors,* where I learned ultra-cool techniques for applying and removing inexpensive makeup.

Being in these bands, choirs, and musicals still wasn't enough; I bought a letter jacket and had my mom sew the names of these activities onto the back, along with the letters I'd received for my participation. Walking through the halls in my oversized letter jacket—an orange and black billboard advertising myself to the bullies and the frightening shop kids who used smokeless tobacco—I'd hear comments ranging from "Band and drama? Who puts that on a coat?" to the more direct "What a homo." Not to worry, though. I never got physically attacked. Nothing staves off a beating from jocks like a toothy smile and an energetic display of "jazz hands."

Performing music and assuming the personalities of characters came naturally to me. I assumed at the time that it meant I was sort of artistic, rather than sort of autistic, but as it turns out, I'm both. The former quality drew people to me, and the latter seemed to push them away. In the ebb and flow of peers, there were a few who stuck around and became close friends, the type that would last a lifetime. There was Andy, who played sports and exhibited genius at every turn. There was Delemont, who was also circus music with feet. And there was Kristen.

A year older than me, and a million times cooler and more popular, Kristen was a pretty, perfectly assembled, athletic blonde who almost always had a cheerful smile on her face. To me the other students were little more than outfits with faces that clogged doorways between classes, but to Kristen they were all friends of varying closeness. She had a singular warmth and capacity for fun that pulled people to her. I was one of them.

Our connection was immediate and seemed to be the result of a mutual appreciation for silliness. We found humor in exactly the same things—and she was one of maybe three people for whom that was true. Gags from Leslie Nielsen movies, the way our gym teacher cleared his throat over the intercom, Paula Abdul—it was fun to laugh about these things with someone, especially someone as wowing as Kristen.

Early in my freshman year, during a rehearsal for *Annie,* I watched as a remarkably arrogant kid bonked his nose against his own knee while working with the choreographer. He (the kid) had been rude to me a number of times ("Is that all you do, Finch? Mimic the sounds you hear over the intercom?"), so witnessing his blunder was deliciously satisfying. In a perfect world, the only sound accompanying his gaffe would have been a toot from a good ole-fashioned bicycle horn, but instead Peckerhead just let out this tiny yelp. He quickly righted himself, covered his nose with his hand, and allowed his face to betray nothing—no pain, no annoyance, nothing—and then he sat like that for the remainder of the rehearsal. Kristen had seen it, too, and we exchanged delighted glances, silently saying to each other, *Yes, that really just happened.* From then on, all I ever had to do to make her laugh was to erase any expression from my face and cover my nose. I'd walk past her chemistry classroom this way, and I'd hear her laugh from her seat in the back row. I'd wave to her in the cafeteria and she'd cover her nose, while her friends asked her what she was doing.

Kristen also observed things about me that my other friends didn't seem to notice. She was, for example, the first and only person to recognize my complete inability to walk out of time with music. Entering the auditorium while the pit band warmed up before rehearsal, I'd cross in front of the stage and take my regular seat in perfect step with the music. If they were rehearsing a slower ballad, it might take me a minute to get to my seat; faster tempos got me there sooner. If the music stopped before I got to my seat, I'd lurch forward and dash the rest of the way. Everyone but Kristen seemed oblivious to this. She'd laugh, saying, "Oh, David James, you just kill me." (I never knew why she called me by my first and middle names, but she was the only person who did, and I loved it.)

Talking to anybody else was usually a depleting chore; conversation was disruptive and I avoided it whenever possible. But Kristen made it something to look forward to. Seeing her in the hallways was exciting, hanging out with her in the music room was calming. I didn't have to work as hard with her. Sitting next to me in the auditorium during rehearsals, she would keep a stream of conversation flowing that I could actually get into. When I grew shy and couldn't keep up, she would do something to lighten me up—launching a tiny thread of saliva onto the stage, for instance (a maneuver which she referred to as "gleeking"), or removing something from my backpack and asking me about it. "That's quite a calculator! Can it spell my name?" The next day in math class, I'd turn it on to find her name written in variables across the screen: kRiʃtEη. Her matching outfits, her bursts of laughter, her ability to spit on a target from thirty feet. I was hopelessly in like.

I was thrilled when we began hanging out more often during school. Study periods once reserved in my mind for diligent work became hour-long blocks of Kristen Time. A daily note from our choir director excused me from my normal study room, so I could spend time "helping" Kristen in the music library, where she volunteered to organize stacks of sheet music—a bogus responsibility that excused her from her own study hall. Surrounded by cluttered shelves of choral arrangements, we would talk and find ways to make each other laugh. Sometimes, I helped her with homework and in return she prevented me from accomplishing anything academic whatsoever. "See, David James, isn't talking to me more fun than outlining your biology chapters?" *Yes, actually, and you're the only person I can say that about.*

Once, I was cramming for a calculus test when she took my notebook and started quizzing me: "David James, find the derivative of x in this equation . . ." When it occurred to her that she couldn't even pronounce the equation, she laughed and teasingly asked me what all the "squiggly little lines" meant. If anyone else had swiped my cherished math notebook and asked this question, it would have released the pin on a tantrum. But coming from Kristen, it was different. When I tried explaining the purpose and sheer beauty of derivatives and integrals, she got bored and began drawing something in the margin of my notebook.

"Look," she said. "It's Duffy the Wonder Dog!"

She handed the notebook back to me, and there, happily wagging its tail beside my meticulous proof, was a little cartoon version of her dog, Duffy, his superhero dog name written in large, bubbly letters across my solution. The next day I answered one of my extra-credit questions on the test, "Delta x with respect to time is . . . Duffy the Wonder Dog." My dad got angry when I showed him the test. He is not a humorless man; far from it. But he didn't see the humor in wasting valuable points on an exam. Kristen did. I still have the drawing.

Our friendship was platonic. Kristen was so far out of my league that it didn't even occur to me that we might be anything more than friends. But, then again, she *was* hot. I don't know that any high school boy with a hot girl for a friend hasn't from time to time imagined a steamy moment in, say, the girls' dressing room behind the auditorium, while, perhaps, the drama geeks were starting their vocal warm-ups.

Can you help me bustle this costume, David?

But the director is starting vocal warm-ups. They'll know we're missing.

Ooh, it will be so dangerous. Glue your mustache on and take me.

Just saying.

I had successfully hosed down any thoughts ignited by my own sexual imagination by the time Kristen started going out with Mike. This was during her junior year, his senior year, my sophomore year. Mike played first-chair alto saxophone in the school bands with me, and I thought I had him pegged. Earrings, muscles, attitude, and he could probably grow a beard—this guy was definitely too cool for me. But when Kristen was around, Mike opened up and I learned that he was as kind and genuine as she was. He was able to draw me out of myself, just like Kristen, and we eventually became friends, too. He taught me mind-blowing sax techniques (do not read that incorrectly) that I never would have learned during my own weekly lessons. And we traded stories about our unusual hobbies—mine included halter-breaking cattle and making dioramas, while he dabbled in coonskin caps and burying machinery in the ground, a snowmobile being his crowning achievement. "I know how to pick my men," Kristen would say, laughing.

When Mike left for college a year later, he jokingly asked me to take care of Kristen for him, a responsibility that I took very seriously in my own Asperger syndrome–y way.

When Kristen came down with the chicken pox during her senior year, for instance, I showed up at her door to surprise her with a get-well kit. A kit that included a new butter dish (just because), a handful of batteries (why not), and my own personal copy of *When Harry Met Sally*. (I was crazy about Nora Ephron movies—just one more thing to make me the coolest kid in school.) I'd always found that movie to be good medicine, and it seemed to work wonders for Kristen as well.

"Thank you for coming over," she said when it was time to go home. "And thanks for my butter dish and batteries. Only you . . ." She laughed.

I covered my nose with my hand, made my face go blank, and told her that I had a wonderful time helping her feel better. She covered her nose and said she'd consider getting the chicken pox more often. With that, I scurried off to my car, clutching my videotape to my chest.

Coolest kid in school.

When Kristen went away to college, we didn't see each other as much. Still, our friendship grew stronger. I would call her with funny stories, and she would call me just to see how I was doing. During holidays and summer breaks, she and Mike and I would get together and hang out. But I no longer needed to take care of her for Mike. She had sorority sisters and loads of friends. She had college and graduate school. Then Mike proposed, and suddenly she had a fiancé. Then just as suddenly, one day, she didn't.

A few months before she and Mike were to be married, he and his brother, Jason, died in a car accident. Kristen's friends from college took turns staying with her at her parents' house for the first few weeks after the accident. I had just graduated from college in Florida and had returned to Illinois to begin my career as an engineer a few months prior. I visited Kristen whenever I could, my presence little more than a reminder of support. I had no idea how to console someone, even my close friend. I wanted to take care of her but when it counted most I was at a loss. I also felt strange because I had witnessed the accident.

I was living alone at the time, in a suburban apartment across the street from Jason and his fiancée, Lisa, who was out with Kristen on the night of the accident. It was late at night and I wasn't yet asleep when I heard the screeching tires, the jarring impact, and the sickening drone of a car horn that couldn't stop blaring. I scrambled out of bed and ran to my patio, where I called 911. I couldn't see the wreck from where I was standing, and I was hopeful that it sounded worse than it actually was. I waited outside in my underwear until the emergency vehicles arrived, and then I said a prayer for the victims and returned to bed, shivering from the adrenaline and the cold November air.

I learned the next morning that the accident I'd heard was Mike and Jason's and that neither of them had survived. Jason died immediately, Mike a few hours later in the hospital in a deep coma, with Kristen at his side, telling him that if he needed to go, then she would be okay. And then he went. And she wasn't okay.

A few months later, Kristen moved in with Lisa, across the street from my apartment. Often she didn't want to see friends, but when she did I made sure to be available. I'd meet her at the park one afternoon and then I might not hear from her for a month or two. I tried to do what Tom Hanks or Billy Crystal might have done for Meg Ryan were it a Nora Ephron film—I offered my company, without expecting her to want it. It was a tactic that prevented me from leaving more than three or four silly messages on her voice mail at a time and allowed me to pretend as though no time had passed when she finally called.

What brought our friendship back to life was, strangely, my girlfriend at the time. Funny how the complete disintegration of one relationship can salvage another. Andrea was a beautiful Italian cellist with hair that spiraled down to her shoulders in tight curls. She got my humor and didn't complain when I'd listen to the same music albums over and over. She was also the only girlfriend of mine Kristen had ever liked, and when it seemed as though Andrea and I weren't clicking anymore, she urged me—even coached me—to make it work.

"This week, I think you should make time to talk with Andrea," she told me one evening over a cup of coffee. "Tell her you feel distant and that you don't know why. Tell her that you feel there's a problem and that you want to work it out with her."

It had been more than a year since the accident, and Kristen was finally starting to seem okay. Not happy yet, not at peace, but okay. All things considered, I was happy for okay.

"That sounds like a good plan," I said, balling up little shreds of brown paper napkin. "I'll try that."

"Try not to overthink it," Kristen said, eyeing the balls of shredded napkin. "Just talk to her. See where the conversation goes, the way you do with me. You two will figure it out."

That night was the first of what would become a standing Tuesday-evening engagement: the two of us getting together for overpriced coffee and free therapy. Each week, we took turns dishing to each other about our respective circumstances. She would listen patiently while I overanalyzed my love life, and because I lacked the normal social skills that might prevent a person from prying, I turned out to be a great conversational partner when she needed to talk about Mike. Unlike most people, I wasn't intimidated by Kristen's sadness and she found it refreshing to be able to open up and speak candidly with someone.

At the end of each session, we would prescribe little assignments for each other. I tried to suggest fun activities to keep her amused, to bring the joy back into her life. Fortunately, acting selfishly as a means of preserving happiness was second nature to me, so I was good at coming up with suggestions. I often encouraged her to go shopping, her favorite pastime. Within a few weeks, she had acquired a second wardrobe. "Spring is just around the corner," she said with a laugh one night, joining me at Starbucks with two armfuls of shopping bags. Most of my other suggestions—taking vacations, journaling, visiting with friends—produced equally positive results.

Kristen's assignments for me, however, were not as successful. I joined her for our tenth cup of coffee with the news that Andrea and I had broken up. We were good on paper—logically it made sense—but it didn't work. Love and logic don't always see eye to eye.

As Kristen and I grew closer, our Tuesday evenings grew longer. We were often the last people to leave the coffee shop, and we started finding it difficult to say good night to each other. What began as coffee once a week became coffee twice a week. Then three times a week plus dinner. Most nights, we chatted and laughed out loud, but other nights we'd people-watch or read books together. Sometimes, we would simply drive around in her car and talk. I would do my best to follow the conversation, but often I was distracted—pleasantly—by the scent of her perfume, the closeness of her body. The way she looked in her workout clothes, or how she would ask me to steer while she re-formed her ponytail. Things that themselves were not new to me but that I had begun noticing more. Things that I'd think about long after we'd said good night.

We began talking on the phone every day, and she would occasionally send me little cards thanking me for making her laugh, for making her feel good about herself, for helping her to be excited about life again. I started making opportunities to see her throughout the day. If I knew that she was going shopping after work, I would sneak out of my office and drive to the mall just so that we could accidentally bump into each other as I casually strolled past Ann Taylor—because what guy doesn't browse women's fashions at three thirty in the afternoon on a weekday?

I was also doing everything I could to stifle logical thinking. Logical thinking prevents us from making catastrophic mistakes. We don't pick fights with bears. We don't lick a hot stove more than once. And, if we're relying solely on logic, we don't fall in love with our best friends. Logic by itself wouldn't let us do such a thing—to jeopardize a close, meaningful relationship for the sake of romance. But feelings have a way of defeating rational thought.

One night in May, Kristen and I met at our usual spot. She had recently gone on vacation and I was eager to hear about her trip. We took our favorite seats beside the fireplace—a pair of plush, oversized chairs that we liked to pull close together, so that our knees almost touched. Kristen always seemed to look just right in hers, easing herself naturally into the comfort, kneading her shoulders against the seat back, and crossing her legs.

That night, as usual, I was having a hard time settling in and looking normal. While I had come to know it as my regular chair, it was still a public chair, and there really was no telling who might have settled into it before me. *Gross folks, probably.* The dander and oils of the masses had been embedded deep into the velveteen upholstery so I was reluctant to remove my coat and settle back, fearful that I might absorb the gook of strangers. Kristen enjoyed a good chuckle watching me as I tried to get comfortable.

She looked especially attractive that evening. Her dark blue jeans and thin cashmere sweater, her high-heeled sandals. It all worked. Suddenly, I was right back in the high-school dressing room, eluding the mandatory vocal warm-ups and gluing on my mustache.

Her clothes, though, were no match for her suntan, which she had gotten on her trip to San Diego. When I commented on it, she gently pulled aside the neck of her sweater and used her fingertips to trace the narrow tan line along her shoulder and neck. *Oh, schwing.* Sliding her fingers back and forth, grinning toward the ceiling, she whispered, "Not here so much . . . Or here . . . But right here." This was a line from *Tommy Boy,* one of our favorite movies, and as she said it, with her delicate fingertips tracing her collarbone, I couldn't imagine liking anyone more than her.

She laughed and started telling me about her trip. My focus shifted between what she was saying and the delicate wisp of blond hair that had fallen lazily over her eye. The beach was nice; she befriended a duck that was living behind her hotel; she met a guy. My ears perked up.

"I beg your pardon?"

He was, she explained, a lot like me. "Only not as funny as you. Or maybe not as cute? I don't know. Not as *something* as you."

Go on.

"We met on the plane and had the best time talking . . ." I chugged half my coffee, trying to look casual. *Sounds like a douche. Please don't hook up with this boner and get married and move away and stop being friends with me.*

"We spent a whole day together at the zoo . . ." I folded a napkin into a flimsy paper airplane, trying to look casual. *Zoo? What? Please don't hook up with this boner and get married and move away and stop being friends with me.*

"We exchanged numbers when we got back to Chicago, but of course he hasn't called me . . ." *Please, please, please don't hook up with this boner and—Wait a second.*

"Boner Boy didn't call you?" I asked, trying to conceal my happiness.

Kristen wasn't even interested in Boner Boy, or "Ryan," as she called him. It was, she told me, simply the thrill of allowing herself to flirt with someone without feeling guilty about it.

"It was just nice to know that I *could* flirt, should I happen to find myself attracted to someone." She gazed at me for a moment, and I forgot how to breathe.

After ratcheting up my courage, I said, "Tell me about your ideal guy."

She described him as being engaging, funny, sweet, completely devoted to her. "Oh, and he'd have to know how to order my coffee," she added coyly.

Ohhhhhhhhhhhhhhhhhh boy.

My heart raced as she adjusted herself in her chair, crossing her legs, letting her lovely shoe dangle from her toes. Her hair spilled over her fingers as she rested her face in her hand, smiling at me.

"Tell me about your ideal woman," she said.

My answer, in its entirety, was sitting right in front of me. I just didn't know if I was reading the situation correctly.

Are we really doing this?

I was pretty sure that we were, but then again, I can't always tell when people are flirting with me and when they're just being nice. When I used to play in bands in college, girls would ask me during bar gigs if I wanted to get a drink with them, and I'd decline, raising my cup and saying, "No, thanks. I've already got my 7-Up and orange juice." If a waitress brought a check with a smiley face drawn on it I'd think, *Wow, smiley face . . . That's pretty forward. Does she want me to call her?* I need things to be black-and-white.

Kristen's eyes locked on mine, bringing me back. She smiled.

"Well, if you're asking . . ."

"I am," she said softly.

That moment reminded me what it meant to feel alive—my face getting hot, my mouth stammering, my words sounding not even remotely poetic. It all somehow led to more amazing moments that evening: going to her house afterward, talking all night about how our friendship was changing and how exciting it felt. Kissing her, and waking up the next morning on her couch, wrapped in her arms.

The euphoria continued, and we were certain it would last. There were trips to Minnesota, Utah, Wisconsin. There were hundreds of restaurants. There were discussions about how lucky we were to have each other. There was a single "I love you" that opened the door to countless more. There were flowers and family introductions and an engagement ring, and still more discussions about how lucky we were to have each other. There was our first house. There were photographers to book and a wedding cake to order. And finally, there were wedding vows.

All this because some doofus bonked his nose against his knee. *Yes, our wedding pictures seem to say, that really happened.*

It's our third anniversary. Much has changed since the silly days of high school and the euphoria of dating. We're sitting in a fancy restaurant. Our chairs aren't squeezed together—instead, they seem miles apart. There's no fireplace, and by tomorrow morning, I will have forgotten what Kristen is wearing. The last few rolls of sushi remain on the platter, illuminated by a candle. My small saucer of soy is almost empty, just some bits of rice and wasabi mingling in the shallow pool. We're supposed to be celebrating but we haven't spoken much. Work. Our baby. Building the new house. People at other tables are chattering, smiling, drinking. I look up to ask if something is wrong, and Kristen is biting her lip, her eyes welling with tears, trying to focus on anything in the restaurant that isn't me.

It's not working. Any of it. Our marriage, it seems, is over.

"What is there to say?" she asks. She looks at me and starts sobbing.

I hand her a napkin, saying nothing.

"I don't know when things got bad," she says, wiping tears from under her eyes. "I feel like I've lost you and I don't know what will bring you back." She chews her lip as she organizes her thoughts. "You're just so cynical and dismissive and checked-out. It's constant. And it's not supposed to be this hard . . ." She can't continue. Her voice is strange, her face is strange—she is consumed with grief.

I'm annoyed that she's doing this right now, but not surprised. This is the first time we've bothered to talk to each other in weeks. What's surprising is how little emotion I feel at this moment. By the time I'm able to process all this, I will feel an overwhelming sadness. But right now, in the moment, I feel almost nothing.

People are looking at us now—first at her, then at me. *Just celebrating our third anniversary, folks. Nothing to see here.*

We are not consciously aware of it this evening, as we sit face-to-face in separate worlds, but Kristen is mourning a loss again. This time it's different. She has my body to hold. It's right here. She can hear me, see me, touch me, feel me. But she doesn't want to do any of those things. Embracing me now would be like embracing a stranger. It's our special friendship that has died, our once deep emotional connection now little more than a distant, if consoling, memory.

I sit back in my seat and wait as she composes herself. She has every reason to be sobbing right now. She is disappointed in me—I'm not the person she thought she was marrying three years ago. I'm not her friend. But I have nothing to say to her that will radically shift our course and get us back on track, because I'm disappointed, too. I'm disappointed in her for not being the woman I'd thought she'd magically become as soon as we were married: the portrait of domestic excellence, the perfect stay-at-home mom fulfilled by her duties and her love for her somewhat quirky husband. The woman I hadn't even known I wanted.

There are no pictures of us on the walls at home, there are no moments of tenderness after a satisfying day of taking care of the baby, there are no clean dishes in the cupboards. There is only resentment. And all this resentment between us certainly explains all the sex we're not having—and this, in turn, does nothing to combat the ever-mounting resentment. Not only are we no longer friends, we are no longer lovers. Now we are just . . . married. *Cheers!*

We never would have—never *could* have—imagined that our relationship would look like this back when we were just friends meeting for coffee. We had no idea that we would someday forget how to be friends. We hadn't planned on assigning new titles to each other, much less that each new title would bear such hefty expectations. My friend Kristen would become my girlfriend Kristen. The word *friend* would vanish from the title when Kristen's boyfriend, Dave, would become her husband, Dave. We didn't know how detached and distant we would feel from each other after three confusing years of marriage. I didn't know how lost and defeated Kristen's eyes would look in our fourth year of marriage, when she'd tell me, "I don't even know why we decided to get married."

Our third anniversary wasn't what we'd planned, and, sadly, neither was our fourth. But thanks to my Asperger's diagnosis, which allowed me to take a step back and look at our situation with new understanding, our fifth anniversary looked promising. *I'm not an asshole. I don't mean to be difficult. I can fix this.* This knowledge gave me the courage to honestly assess the state of our union, as fractured as it was. There was almost no communication, as our conversations only led to arguments. The responsibilities of working and raising children and being married to an underdeveloped man left Kristen exhausted all the time. I never offered to help. I had no idea how to be a parent. Or a husband, for that matter.

Though it was difficult to admit these things to myself, the naked honesty was refreshing and strengthened my resolve to get in there and fix everything. While I couldn't envision the steps we'd need to take to get there, I found it rather easy to summarize the end goal: *We have to get back to being friends.*

I committed myself to this concept—to this Best Practice— without any clue as to where we should begin. It felt like quail hunting with my dad on the farm where I grew up. Quail are these smallish game birds that huddle together under the cover of tall grass as predators approach. They don't fly until it's absolutely necessary. I'd take a step and suddenly, out of nowhere, there would be a half-dozen birds in my face, launching themselves into the sky, while my dad yelled, *"Shoot! Shoot!"* from across the field. I could see the birds, I could count them, but I could never get the hang of setting myself, drawing my gun, aiming, and firing before they flew out of range. Dad would laugh and roll his eyes, and I'd stand there trembling, wondering, *Which one was I supposed to shoot?* Such were the problems in my marriage. Problems were everywhere, but which one should I attack first? What was the first step to getting our friendship back?

Chapter 2

Use your words.

Determined to find out what that first step would be, I sat down with Kristen in our family room about a week after my diagnosis, along with my notebook and pages upon pages of information on autism spectrum conditions that I'd printed from various Internet sources. The kids were upstairs napping, and at that time of day the sunlight fell directly upon our television screen, making it impossible to watch. Kristen was relaxing with a celebrity gossip magazine and eating black olives straight from the can. I plopped down beside her on the couch and arranged my materials neatly before her on the coffee table.

"What's all this?" she asked, leafing through my stack of papers.

"This is all the Asperger's stuff about me that we need to fix if we want to save our marriage. You're the expert, and I need you to show me where we're going to start."

I felt proud: *I'm doing it! I'm stepping up! I'll be Asperger's-free in no time!* Kristen nodded thoughtfully, then shuffled the papers together and set them aside. Then, for the third or fourth time that week, she reminded me, "We can work together to fix our marriage, Dave. This isn't about fixing you."

I opened up my notebook and jotted down, *Fixing our marriage is about working together and managing my behaviors. Not fixing me.*

"That's good," I said. "Keep going."

Kristen suggested that we begin by working on communication. Our ability to talk to each other, she told me, was paramount, yet we'd been struggling with it for years. When it came to discussing anything other than what was for dinner, we fell apart.

"There are many things that we need to address in our relationship," she said, "but we won't get anywhere if we can't communicate with each other. Communication has to come first, then the other pieces will start to fall into place."

I wrote the word *communication* in my notebook and said that I agreed, especially considering that she was an expert on speech and communication disorders.

"Those aren't exactly the issues we'll be dealing with," she said. "It's not like you're nonverbal."

"No, really. I read about it." I searched through my stack of papers. "People with Asperger syndrome have difficulty communicating. Hang on, it's in one of these printouts."

I found the article I was looking for and handed it to Kristen. Kristen, the actual expert on speech and communication disorders. She frowned at the title and handed the paper back to me. It was full steam ahead on the Asperger's Express, but apparently I was the only one riding.

It was true, she explained, that people on the autism spectrum tend to have difficulty navigating social interactions. Effective communication requires more than an exchange of words; conversational partners must adequately read each other's emotions, reactions, and underlying motives, and they must be able to understand each other's perspective. These abilities are a product of social intuition, a resource with which people with Asperger's tend to be relatively ill equipped. But that, Kristen told me, was something we could worry about later.

"For now, don't worry about the implications of your diagnosis," she said. "Yes, you have Asperger syndrome and that's part of the barrier. But let's face it, Dave, you can communicate. What's holding you back are thirty years of habits. We need to practice talking to each other, that's all."

Though she didn't spell it out for me, I understood exactly what Kristen meant by thirty years of habits. Growing up, I was never taught the importance of healthy, therapeutic discourse. I was discouraged from talking about negative feelings toward other people, especially family members. If you can't say anything nice, don't say anything at all—this old chestnut was both a philosophy and a firmly enforced rule in my family. My brother and I were not allowed to argue with each other, nor were we encouraged to voice any differences of opinion with authority figures (especially my parents). The airing of grievances, we were told, amounted to whining—"bellyaching," as my dad called it—and nothing irritated my parents more than bellyaching. If we did have a personal issue with someone we loved, we were supposed to internalize the attendant frustration and hope that, like a virus or a stomachache, it would simply run its course. This kept emotions from boiling over, but just barely. It kept the house quiet, anyway.

My parents led this crusade by example. If we had a family crest, it might bear the image of four smiling faces sweeping animosity under a rug. Which had always been fine with me, truth be told. As a child, I never (not even once) saw my parents argue. Sometimes I saw my friends' parents argue viciously—right in front of me, their invited guest—and the tension it created was unbearable. *This family sucks,* I'd think. *I can't be friends with this kid.* But that wouldn't have happened at my house. My mom and dad clearly loved each other, so as I understood it, people who loved each other never argued.

That's not to say that my parents had nothing to argue about. Far from it. They were married, and like anyone else they must have had their own needs and disappointments. I remember my mom being angry on occasion, indignantly throwing silverware into drawers, but she never told any of us what was bothering her. Not me or my brother, and certainly not my dad. And I remember noticing how my mom's fits coincided with my dad's own bad moods—often I found that if I had to avoid my mom, it was best to stay away from my dad, too. Beyond that, I never thought anything of it. I didn't understand that they were unwilling to sit down and talk about whatever the problem was, just as their parents had been, and their parents before them. And now me.

"My parents never talked about their feelings," I said to Kristen, "but they have been married almost forty years now and they're getting happier all the time."

"That's because their system works for them. But look at us. Can you honestly tell me you think it's working, all this silence?"

I sat back and propped my feet upon the coffee table, thinking of all the vacations that had been ruined over the years because I had chosen to brood for days over an issue rather than spend ten minutes confronting it. Of all the holidays and parties rendered awkward because Kristen and I hadn't seen the point in talking to each other. The countless times Kristen had urged me to share what was on my mind and I'd simply said, "Forget it," and walked away from her, convinced she wouldn't understand.

"No," I said, "it's not working."

Kristen pointed out, too, how damaging it is to withhold things like resentment, anger, and frustration. That doing so had already taken a toll on our relationship and that she worried it would eventually make me sick if I kept it up. I nodded and wrote down *swallowing anger = swallowing poison*. The other problem with saying "Forget it," she told me, was that I wasn't someone who knew how to forget about things that were bothering me. I took another note: *She is onto you.*

"If you could actually let go of an issue and put it behind you, then okay, I'd say we could just forget it once in a while," she said. "But you retain things. If something bothers you, it gets stuck inside your head and you wind up stomping around the house in a terrible mood for days and you make everyone else miserable in the process. Most of the time, it's something we could easily sort out if you'd just take that first step and talk to me about it."

I agreed, though I couldn't help but feel disappointed. It was clear that we had become the couple that couldn't communicate with each other. Kristen and I were never supposed to be that couple.

Before we were married we always talked, and though we had different opinions about things, we never argued. She was still that girl in the high school auditorium who kept the conversation flowing, who kept my mind and my mouth involved, the girl who played with my calculator and asked me about math.

Adulthood hadn't changed our friendship much. Our conversations centered on lighter musings: "If you could live anywhere, where would it be?" or "I once saw a guy put his entire fist inside his mouth." Even heavier topics didn't bother me back then because whatever we talked about bore little consequence to me personally. We were just friends, after all. ("*Of course* I think you should quit your job and go backpacking through Costa Rica. Why *wouldn't* you?") Perhaps most important, when we were friends it was perfectly acceptable for me to be egocentric. This quality actually seemed to make me more interesting as a conversational partner, as I was her only pal who related everything back to himself—something that, ironically, had always made her laugh: "On second thought, don't go to Costa Rica because (a) I'll miss you and (b) I don't want to have to water your plants."

Then we married each other and things changed. When you're in love, you can't beat the notion of two souls uniting, two lives becoming forever one. Sooner or later, though, the romance fades. One day you realize you are two souls united . . . but there's only one cupcake left in the Tupperware container in the fridge. That's when reality sets in: *We're going to have to deal with stuff, and it might not be easy.* Whether Kristen and I were ready for it or not (which, clearly, we were not), our relationship changed after we were married, and the nature of what we needed to express changed with it: *How shall we handle our finances? What's your philosophy on child rearing? What do you* mean *you have interests and aspirations beyond being my wife?!*

We weren't alone. Most couples don't consider or discuss these types of things until they have to, until they're both staring at the same cupcake, wondering what they've gotten themselves into. Kristen and I would learn that these were the things we would have to talk about if we wanted our marriage to work. As we got farther into married life, we'd also discover that I was particularly unprepared—unequipped, it seemed—to do that.

When issues arose—and believe me, when you're married and have a mild form of autism you're not even aware of, things tend to come up—I couldn't talk about them constructively with Kristen. That would have required me to have the ability to understand her point of view, to consider her needs rather than mine. Which I didn't, and couldn't. Not only were we dealing with issues common to every marriage, we were also forced to deal with extremely bizarre challenges that plague relationships for people on the autism spectrum: my daily routines, my obsessive tendencies, my unwillingness to participate in social events.

When Kristen and I needed to talk about these things, we would almost always end up having an argument; she couldn't believe the things she had to talk to me about ("When we have company over, it's not okay for you to get in your car and leave for an hour, Dave. Don't you understand that?"), and I couldn't handle the reality of constantly—there's no other way of saying this—fucking up. I didn't *mean* to spoil the parties. I didn't *mean* to cast a shadow over the entire holiday weekend because my schedule had been thrown out of whack. It just happened that way, so to Kristen I looked like a jerk, which seemed completely unfair to me.

The condition I was born with led us to these moments of heated discussion and profound misunderstanding. But the way I was raised dictated how I handled them. Because I firmly believed that arguments were symptomatic of doomed relationships, I would refuse to participate. It didn't matter how small the disagreements were. Deciding when to have kids or selecting a laundry detergent—if we disagreed, I couldn't handle it. I would get frustrated. By the end of our first year of marriage, I had learned that voicing frustration led to arguments, so I wouldn't say anything. *Fine,* I'd think, *go with the generic detergent that I wouldn't be caught dead using. I guess it doesn't matter which detergent I prefer.* I would shut down and brood, or pout, as Kristen would say. (And, oh, how that word *pout* pissed me off.) As coping strategies go, brooding was one of the worst; Kristen could see right through it. She'd see that I was angry, she'd know *why* I was angry, and yet I would deny my feelings, insisting that nothing was wrong. Then I'd try to prove my point, I suppose, by stomping around and acting mad for a few days. Being short with her and mean to salesclerks. Throwing a temper tantrum, in other words.

By our second year of marriage, Kristen no longer saw the point in trying to get me to talk. She no longer appreciated the daily challenges and constant feuding. She no longer saw me as the wonderful man with whom she could discuss anything; instead, she saw me as this temperamental man-child who couldn't handle the demands of real life. And who wouldn't love going to bed with *that* guy every night?

Looking back, even I find it hard to believe that Kristen and I lived like this for the first five years of our marriage. Not five weeks or five months. The first five years. Let alone that our marriage survived long enough for us to turn things around. My diagnosis had made things click for us. It allowed both of us to take a deep breath, wipe the slate clean, and start thinking about our relationship in a different light. It allowed us to think about why we had stopped communicating years before and what we could do to start talking again.

The key to becoming a couple that could communicate was to communicate. (I know this is tricky stuff—try to stay with me, here.) And the key to communicating, Kristen told me, was to use my words. She used this approach when dealing with Emily, our two-year-old. Kristen had taught Emily sign language long before Emily was able to speak. She knew that many of Emily's temper tantrums were the result of her inability to express herself; if she wanted more banana, for example, she had no way of saying it. But she could sign it. Whenever Emily wanted something and started getting frustrated, Kristen would tell her, "Use your words." Then Emily would calm down and press her little hands together, saying, "more," before rubbing her chest, saying, "please." Emily quickly learned that tantrums led nowhere, but communication produced results. It was an important concept for our daughter to grasp, and at thirty years of age I was going to have to do the same.

The first opportunity came only a few days after Kristen and I agreed to start working on communication. It was Kristen's day off, and we thought it would be fun to meet for lunch near my office with the kids. We had never done that before, and I was excited to show them where I worked. At home I wasn't very impressive, but at the office people listened to me, and I wanted the kids to see that. Best of all, one of my coworkers was likely to high-five me right in front of them. For once, my family could see that I was totally the man.

When Kristen arrived, she pulled into a visitor parking space and called me at my desk to let me know she was there.

"Come on up," I said, peering down at our car from my fourth-story window, trying to sound indifferent. "I'll meet you by the reception desk." People were always milling around the reception area, and I figured at least one of them would give me that crucial high five the moment Kristen and the kids stepped off the elevator.

"Really?" Kristen said. "We're all buckled in. It would be a lot easier if you just came down."

"But I wanted the kids to see where I work. I thought they'd enjoy it."

"Well, Parker is gnawing on his foot and Emily thinks we're driving to Disney World. I doubt they would understand they're in Daddy's office."

I felt a swell of disappointment as I looked around my cubicle, which I'd spent all morning cleaning in preparation for their visit. "Fine," I said, "I'll be right down."

At the restaurant, I had a little temper tantrum. I ignored Kristen's attempts at making conversation and went out of my way to be rude to our waiter. I felt I'd been made a fool and I couldn't let it go, but I wasn't going to bring it up and ruin our lunch with an argument. Instead, we sat for fifteen minutes in that familiar, awkward silence, watching Parker as he worked his way through some dry Cheerios and Emily as she scribbled on her place mat with a crayon. Finally, our food arrived.

"Are you going to tell me what's the matter, Dave?" Kristen asked, cutting Emily's chicken and broccoli into tiny, bite-size pieces.

I didn't say anything, so she took my plate away and fired me a look that said, *We are not doing this today.*

"Give it back," I said.

Kristen smiled and shook her head. "Not until you start talking."

I quickly looked around the restaurant, hoping that none of my colleagues were there to witness what was shaping up to be a defining moment in my life.

"I'm serious," I said, stifling a nervous grin. "Give it to me."

Without taking her eyes off me, Kristen plucked a french fry from my plate and popped it in her mouth. "Mmm, this is *so* good. You should try some."

I folded my arms and sat back in my seat, scowling at her. Emily started to ask her a question, but Kristen wouldn't break eye contact. "Just a minute, Emily," she said, interrupting. Slowly, she held out my plate, and when I reached for it, she pulled it back playfully.

"Gimme the damn burger," I said.

"I will. Here, take it."

She did it again and started laughing. She had me now, and all I could do was laugh in return. Finally, she handed back my plate, saying, "Now, use your words."

It took a little more coaxing, but I finally explained what had been bothering me. I told Kristen that I'd cleaned my desk and that I'd planned on giving them a tour of the building. When I got to the part about the kids seeing me high-five a coworker, we both busted up laughing.

"Well, I'm sorry that we foiled your plan." Kristen chuckled. "Why didn't you just say that to begin with? We could have been enjoying ourselves this whole time, but instead you just sat there, brooding. That's why you have to use your words."

I admitted that I felt reluctant to submit to the process of communication when it mattered. I understood that we had to talk about things, but it seemed like an exercise that would invite a lot of arguments. "I don't want to fight all the time," I explained.

"Well, these little meltdowns are way more toxic and dramatic than the occasional argument," Kristen said. "I can handle an argument, but I don't do drama."

As we ate our lunches, I noticed that I felt more relaxed having talked through my issue. My jaw wasn't clenched, my shoulders weren't tight. I was having lunch with my family in a crowded restaurant and I felt happy. That's when I realized we had just experienced our first victory. When the check arrived, I wrote a note to myself on the back of the receipt: *Say it, don't show it. Talking = productive. Showing = drama. Kristen doesn't do drama.* Then I wrote, *Use your words.*

In that moment, I handed myself over to the process. I became more comfortable using words to express myself, Kristen became comfortable sharing her feelings with me in return, and it wasn't long before we started seeing the rewards of our efforts. The most notable being that when something was bothering me—anger over a misunderstanding, interruptions to my daily routine, itchy shirt cuffs—I no longer felt as though anger had a physical hold on me. I no longer felt isolated, misunderstood, or hopeless. I could simply talk and know that Kristen would help me through it, no matter how big or small the problem was.

The change didn't happen overnight, of course, nor did it happen easily. The first obstacle we encountered was that I had no concept of the subtle, procedural aspects of communication—the unwritten rules of engagement—all of which had to be learned and recorded into my Journal of Best Practices. Not only did I have to learn how to express myself, I had to learn *when* to express myself. "Yes, we need to talk about our feelings," Kristen whispered to me in the bathroom at my parents' house on Easter, "but not right now at the dinner table in front of all your relatives." *Ask if it's a good time to talk,* I wrote later that evening, just beneath *If you can't tell whether you've offended her, just ask* and *Apologies do not count when you shout them.*

Another challenge lay in all the misdirected rage we had to deal with. Not Kristen's rage, of course, but mine. She had been right; bottling up my anger for three decades had been a mistake. It was as if a dam had burst. Now that we were attempting to deal with things, all the pain of being misunderstood by and misunderstanding others was breaking free. Because of this, not every conversation went smoothly. I would ask Kristen where my phone was, for instance, and within half an hour we would be examining my innermost feelings about that award I received in second grade for having the messiest desk in the classroom. Nevertheless, Kristen maintained her end of the bargain and hung in there with extraordinary patience. More than once I found myself apologizing for hours of constant swearing, yelling, and dramatic weeping, while Kristen stood by like the cartoon coyote whose face had just been blackened by an exploding bomb and replied, "It's fine. It's all in the name of progress."

Asperger's made it difficult for me to read Kristen properly—another roadblock. Using my words was one thing; interpreting hers was something else altogether. Harder still was trying to interpret what she *wouldn't* say. Though I have yet to master this skill, and perhaps never will, I did commit to reaching at least a functional level of mind reading. I eventually got there, but not without months of unnecessary, painful eruptions. My tendency had been to enter into our emotional discussions like a raw nerve; nearly everything could provoke an extreme reaction. Kristen would take a second longer than I thought necessary to answer a question, and I'd explode: "Silent treatment?! Fuck it! I'm outta here." Now that we are aware of my propensity to misread things, Kristen takes these outbursts in stride, while I do my best to preempt them: *Calm down. Don't assume you know what she's thinking. Use your words.*

To overcome all of this, Kristen suggested strategies for recognizing and dealing with my emotions in real time, telling me when I had reacted inappropriately and showing me different ways to respond to my feelings. (Again, but worth repeating, this was something that she had never bargained for.) When I came unglued one evening because the kids had gone to bed late—eight fifteen instead of the normal seven thirty bedtime, pushing my entire evening schedule back forty-five minutes—Kristen sat me down and worked me through it:

"Listen. It's okay for you to expect a certain bedtime, and it's okay for you to get upset. But it is not okay for you to rant and rave in front of the kids when we stay up later than usual. They're absorbing everything you do. They're learning by your example, so if you're not careful we may end up with two little spazzes on our hands."

As I cracked open my notebook to write down some thoughts, she suggested a better way of dealing with bedtime: "If you start feeling freaked out, you have to tell me, 'It's almost bedtime. Let's get them ready.'" Or, she told me, if I really wanted to take a step in the right direction I could simply get the kids ready for bed myself. (Duh.)

While Kristen worked diligently with me on expressing my emotions, I began to take a keen interest in casual conversation. Before we started all of this, the ability to talk casually with people seemed to me to be on a par with the ability to juggle or to do a headstand. As my ability to express myself improved, I couldn't help but think that I could extend this discipline to casual conversation. I figured that could make life easier for me in untold ways. I also suspected that if I were generally better at talking to people, then Kristen would like me more.

But I wasn't born with the gift of gab. Instead, I was born with something along the lines of anti-gab: my instincts don't just inhibit productive interaction, they defeat it altogether. I might laugh at inappropriate times, or meow. I sometimes win my audience over in one sentence and alienate them in the next: "I hope your sister is doing better since her divorce. I mean, let's face it, she was lucky to have found *anyone,* really."

Luckily, my brain does an excellent job of observing people and memorizing and copying their behaviors. Kristen has said that I sometimes resemble someone with a multiple personality disorder and that I should be grateful for it, and I suppose she's right. I use the characteristics I observe in other people to create characters that I can assume at will: Outgoing Man, Boyfriend Guy, Quiet Dude. This ability helps me to seem normal enough to get by in life, but I knew that I could do better, especially considering the progress I'd made in the first couple of months after my diagnosis.

I decided that I needed a role model—someone I could study, from whom I could learn. I had always listened to Howard Stern in the mornings, and if he could earn millions of dollars for making four-hour conversations sound interesting, it seemed a good place to start. I began taking notes about what made Howard so effective at communicating, though this was always at the expense of being on time for work. My boss wanted to know why he could see me sitting in my car in the parking lot at ten o'clock on a Monday morning, nodding my head and scribbling in a notebook. I suppose he thought I should be attending his weekly department meeting, but I had something more important to do: *Howard works methodically through his anecdotes and uses interruptions by others to his advantage. Pacing and flexibility = <u>critical</u>.*

Then I expanded my range. I studied David Letterman, Oprah Winfrey, Regis Philbin. Emulating these talk-show celebrities may sound corny, but these people made conversing look so easy on their shows. These were the leading experts. These were the people from whom I needed to learn.

Because I'm typically on the fringe of a discussion, nodding my head and praying for it to be over, or at least for it to be my turn to talk about something, I am completely fascinated by those who can do it with ease. Watching a great conversationalist in action is, to me, as captivating and entertaining as watching top athletes or ballroom dancers. Great conversationalists engage with their entire bodies. They supplement their words with calculated, expressive eye contact. They don't judge the people they're talking to, but rather encourage honest and open discourse. Great conversationalists ask questions that motivate others to keep speaking, rather than questions that can be answered with a terminating yes or no. When it comes to personal questions, they know the difference between those that are relevant and those that seem creepy and intrusive; they avoid the latter. If they aren't intrinsically interested in a person or a topic, they don't turn around and walk away midsentence like I do. They feign interest, and they do it convincingly: "Now, was this the *first* time your mother had ever been to Duluth?" They finish their sentences, and they know when to move on. In other words, they do everything I don't.

Conversation involves reciprocity and timing—neither of which comes naturally to me. So I absorbed the patterns that emerged between my new role models and their celebrity guests. I learned to integrate the rhythms and the melodies of their voices. And then I'd try out the patterns with various people throughout my day.

I was Regis discussing a recent bus accident with Kristen: "You know, I was watching the news earlier this morning, the coverage of the bus collision, and I have to tell you . . . sometimes tragedy strikes and you wonder how something like this could happen to so many innocent people. My thoughts and prayers are certainly with the victims and their families." Prompting Kristen's "What on earth are you *talking* about?"

I was Howard getting to the bottom of a coworker's love life: "Now, let me back up for just a second, if I may. You said—because we've talked about this in the past, and I think it's an important point, in the sense that . . . you say you need to feel *loved* by women. Would you say this is true? In other words, you feel as though you need a woman to be interested in *you*. Am I right about this? So, when did you start to sense that your girlfriend was interested in you sexually? And I'll tell you why I'm asking . . ." Prompting, "Dude, seriously?"

I was Oprah giving a lecture on digital audio topics to an audience of technology directors and engineering managers: "We're talking today about digital audio technology, a topic which is at the forefront of today's consumer landscape. It's in our *cars,* it's in our *phones,* it's in our *fire alarms* . . . people, and yet, many of us don't realize just how many formats are available. Well, today, we're having a discussion about where some of these audio formats came from, and what we can expect . . . in the not-too-distant future. Let's take a look." This, for some reason, prompted a request for a bathroom break and my boss's quiet recommendation that I tone it down and act more normal.

I was Letterman being overly affable and playfully condescending at a summertime picnic with Kristen's entire family: "Oh, my goodness, what do we have here? Man oh man, I don't care how many times I've said it, I don't care how many bowls I've eaten, I don't care if it's served hot, or cold, or stirred up in the pot there . . . I'll say it again, boys and girls: I love a green bean casserole. Who's with me?" While that line may have garnered Letterman a bass-guitar rip and a rim shot, it got me only a few uneasy chuckles and an extra helping.

I thought I'd come up with a clever strategy, something that I could use in any social situation, but Kristen quickly put an end to it. At home, anyway. It was for the best. Every time she opened her mouth, I would talk-show her to death. "What, am I on set now?" she'd ask. "Can I talk a few minutes longer or do you need to go to commercial?"

I now use the technique only when Kristen's not around, mostly for business meetings and phone calls. I've even expanded the idea to include behind-the-scenes preparation and research. Successful talk-show hosts always have their material ready—they do their homework and are well-versed in their subject matter. Before any important phone call or meeting, I now take an hour or two—however long it takes, really—to think about and research whatever subject I'll be discussing. It's also helpful to script out a number of possible conversations, using what I feel would be potential questions from the other parties: What do you hope to achieve in this meeting? Who should be involved in this decision? Is the sombrero idea really necessary? It helps me to organize my thoughts and to feel more prepared. More confident.

I use a similar strategy to sort out complex personal issues, often when I'm in the shower. If I need to get to the bottom of something—my true feelings about capitalism, for instance—I interview myself. I become the host and the guest simultaneously, and usually by the time my segment comes to an end, I've made a number of profound personal discoveries.

Kristen, the kids, and I were driving to my parents' house one afternoon a few months after my diagnosis when I pointed out what I felt was the final stumbling block in our quest to improve communication. Namely, I worried that by talking more, we would uncover things about ourselves that were best left unexplored.

"Like what?" she asked.

Without going into specifics, I told her that I knew at some point I'd have to talk about some difficult things: my own feelings of inadequacy, feelings of regret for not being the husband I thought she should have, feelings of disappointment in our marriage. Thoughts that had been occupying my mind for months—some of them for years—and I didn't want to carry them around any longer. They were a burden, and I didn't know if I should consult her, or a doctor, or what.

"Okay," she said, carefully applying some eyeliner in the visor mirror. Apparently my revelation was nothing earth-shattering.

"The thing is," I continued, "I don't know how I can sort out these things without talking to you, and if I can't resolve these particular issues, then we'll always be facing the same problems over and over."

She adjusted the visor and checked her lipstick. "You have to understand that if there's something that's really bothering you, then you can always—no matter what—come to me and discuss it," she said. "We both have issues, and that's why we're doing all of this. So we can talk about it."

"Right," I said. "I'm just afraid that if I open all these doors, then you're going to see some pretty heavy things and . . . you know . . ."

"And what?" she asked, closing the visor. She was looking at me now. Out of nowhere, my eyes started watering up. She grabbed my hand and held it in her lap. "What is it?"

"I'm afraid that if I bring all this shit to you, you're going to think I'm a total freak and leave me, and I swear to God, I can't do this without you. You can't leave me. But I don't know who else to talk to about this stuff." I was crying now, and we were three minutes from my parents' house. *I've got Asperger syndrome, but it doesn't have me!*

"Dave," she said, "first of all, do you know me? You have to know that I will never leave you. For any reason. And second of all, I'm not going to judge you for what's on your mind. I'm willing to talk about anything, especially something that's important to you."

I nodded and watched as the pavement, trees, and rooftops melted and blurred through my tears. "So, it's not crazy to talk to you about my insecurities?"

"No crazier than pretending to be a talk-show host all day long."

I kissed her hand. "I love you so much." We drove a few more minutes, circling the neighborhood in silence while I pulled myself together. There was so much to say, so much to thank her for, and yet, at that moment, so few words I needed to use.

Chapter 3

Get inside her girl world and look around.

N ow that Kristen and I were talking more, it was becoming increasingly clear just how much we had lost touch with each other. Our conversations were often emotional and cathartic, which was necessary for rebuilding our partnership. But there's a lot of friendship to be gained in the little stuff—what's your favorite cheese, how is your project coming along at work, that sort of thing. We needed a respite from therapeutic discussion, but often we found ourselves groping for viable topics.

"Did I tell you that I had lunch with April?" she'd ask.

"Yep."

Half an hour would pass, and Kristen would laugh about something she was reading on her computer.

"What are you reading?" I'd ask.

"Oh, just this thing."

We couldn't seem to find the common ground on which our relationship had begun. I couldn't bring myself to discuss my job, as I never particularly cared for it to begin with. When I did have a story to tell about work, she'd stumble over people's names ("Wait, Ben and Benjamin aren't the same person?"), or she'd get lost in the technical terminology ("So, anyway, I had to discuss thermal dynamics vis-à-vis semiconductor operation with this Six Sigma engineer"). I may as well have been barking like a seal. My standard line of questioning relating to her day usually sounded so mechanical and awkward that she could never quite get into it: "Yeah, it was a good day. Notable? I wouldn't say notable. Quantify it how, Dave? You mean, score it on a scale of one to ten? I guess my day was, like, a six or seven. No, ten being the best. Listen, can I call you later?"

In such chilling moments, when I'd found myself hoping—praying—to get carjacked by Charlie Sheen so that I'd have something to share at dinner, I had to wonder what had gone so wrong. *Are we really this out of sync with each other? When did that happen?*

When Kristen and I were friends, being compatible was easy. We loved driving around, trying to get lost. We loved watching people trip and slam into things. Common ground, it seemed, was everywhere.

As friends, it didn't matter much that Kristen was a girl with very girly interests—things that I knew nothing about. No one in my life was as girly as her. Not even former girlfriends had been so girly. The girls I had dated before Kristen tended to be artsy, outdoorsy—they weren't the sorts of people who would rapidly fan their faces with their hands whenever they became emotional or who enjoyed shopping.

Kristen's girl world was foreign and curious to me, so I paid close attention to it. It was cute, in a way. *My God, how many ponytail holders does a person need?* I wondered once, rooting through her coat pocket for a stick of gum. Spending time with Kristen was one thing, but whenever she threw her girlfriends into the mix, I felt as though I were visiting some remote civilization I'd only read about in *National Geo-*

graphic. "You mean, you *actually* share clothes with each other when you go out? I thought that was a myth."

Kristen's girl world didn't intimidate me until I fell in love with her. I had no insight into that aspect of her life, and suddenly, my ignorance felt like a huge liability. Yes, I had fallen in love with someone who wouldn't think twice about burping in a crowded movie theater, but I had also fallen in love with someone who loved shopping. Someone who knew why certain clothes could and couldn't be worn together. Someone who had sorority sisters; a purse with absurd, almost infinite capacity; and sticky bottles of lotion in the cup holders of her car. Someone who watched MTV reality shows, who applied the word *cute* to everything from babies to belts, who understood what celebrities were talking about during televised red-carpet events. I had no clue what was going on inside her girl world, but I had fallen in love with her and I wanted her to love me back, so I felt an urgency—a motivated desire—to understand it.

My approach to understanding new things has always been to study them exhaustively from a safe, academic distance. If told to book a hotel room, I'll spend hours on the hotel's website and reservation hotline trying to understand the dimensions of the rooms, what the reception area looks like, and the texture of the ceiling ("It's not stucco, is it?"). To others, this seems like a lot of unnecessary work, but to me it pays off in spades when I finally arrive and everything is basically as I'd pictured it: *No surprises, I can relax.*

In an effort to acquaint myself with Kristen's girl world, I began studying *Cosmopolitan* magazine. I had several publications to choose from—*Elle, Marie Claire, Cosmo*—but I knew that Kristen had a subscription to *Cosmo,* so I figured I'd start there.

I skimmed it cover to cover to get a general overview of the subject matter and then started over from the beginning, absorbing each tiny little article, banner, and Dove soap advertisement like a physicist poring over Einstein's notebooks.

Every glossy, frantic page took me deeper into the world of a *Cosmo* girl—that mythical size-zero goddess from a land of orange and pink in which creative sex positions are explored nightly, who is forever finding courage to confront hostile coworkers and toxic friends. While it wasn't exactly a road map to the mind and heart of a real-life young woman, the magazine did provide me with talking points. Nighttime skin-care tips, caring for split ends, how not to hurt a guy's feelings when you hate his cologne. Extensive data that I could use to understand the hemisphere of Kristen's world that I'd been ignoring for so long as a friend.

At first, I took the content at face value. *Gee, what does Kristen's part say about her? Hmm. Right-sided . . . see Gwyneth Paltrow. Okay, Gwyneth Paltrow. Here we go: Kristen comes across as outgoing, flirtatious, and artistic. Holy cow. They're right! What about me? Let's see, left-sided . . . see Hilary Swank. Okay, I'm a leader, I'm smart, assertive, and powerful. Nice. That'll do, Cosmo. That'll do.*

I also made the mistake of trying to understand what women love and hate about men. This little exercise almost drove me mental: *So, women hate to love what they hate about men.* In fact, I found that many of the heavier-hitting articles, the ones with titles like "Should You Try to Hurry Love?" and "The Wild and Wacky Way He Wooed Me," were more diverting than they were helpful. I couldn't picture Kristen writing in to one of these columns, given the types of things that I had been reading: the girl who met her beau—and it's always "beau" in *Cosmo* land—in a drunken fistfight at a party, the girl who fell for her beau after he fished her bracelet out of a public trash can. What would Kristen write about me in *Cosmo*? "I agreed to go to an insect exhibit at the museum with my new beau. Before the big day, he snuck into my closet and glued spiders to my shoes. When I told him it was creepy, he started crying. I guess I like the sensitive ones." I didn't think I was getting an all-access pass into Kristen's point of view with articles like those. *Maybe* Cosmo *doesn't speak for* all *of its subscribers . . .*

I wanted to know more about the day-to-day things: the fabulous exercises, the health benefits of keeping a box of wheatgrass near your bed, and at what time of day a woman's sense of taste is most acute (six P.M., according to "The Body Clock Guide to Better Health," as reported in *Cosmo*). I was starting to piece together mental pictures of Kristen throughout her day. There she was at the gym, adding sizzle to her crunches. There she was in her bedroom, spritzing her wheatgrass with water and shoving it back under her bed. There she was at six P.M., ordering her food carefully, mindful of her heightened sense of taste. It was all starting to click for me.

The sense of discovery was thrilling, and my research became something like a compulsion. I took the magazine to work and labored over it at my desk. Right there, in a section devoted to pleasure, was a four-step guide to giving an awesome head massage. It was intended as a pre-shampoo massage, but I tried it with Kristen once when she had a headache, and she melted in my hands, whispering, "Don't stop. This is amazing." *That'll do*, Cosmo. *That'll do*.

The following week, I rearranged all the objects in my cubicle at work after a late-night discussion of feng shui that left us both convinced that I think best facing southwest. People were curious as to why my computer was sitting atop my lateral file. Had I hung any pictures of Kristen, I would have had something to point to, something that they could have understood. "See?" I might have said. "She's beautiful, and she inspired me." As it was, I was left with only "It's a productivity thing. Now help me move this bookshelf."

While I found it difficult to shoehorn specific articles and subject matter into our conversations ("Oh, speaking of the cutest ways to cover up at the beach . . ."), I did develop a higher-level appreciation for unfamiliar topics. Things like eye makeup tips and tricks, the summer's hottest nail polishes, the reasons a woman *shouldn't* panic about post-sex bleeding. *Hmm, so this is what makes her tick*. I was now armed with knowledge; suddenly Kristen's girl world wasn't as intimidating. Her girliness wasn't to be feared, it was to be appreciated, one more dimension with which to be enamored, and I hopelessly was.

As we grew older, Kristen's tastes changed. *Cosmo* and *Elle* were eventually replaced by *Vogue* and *Shape*. After we got engaged, I snuck copies of *Modern Bride* into the bathroom, and once married, I'd look forward to new issues of *Lucky* magazine. *What might she be wearing this fall?* She became pregnant, and money got tight. *Lucky* magazine was for women who could afford to buy clothes, and then wear them, not for expecting mothers, so *Parenting* magazine it was. Her retail catalogs followed the same trajectory. Victoria's Secret stopped coming around, leaving room in the mailbox for Mimi Maternity and Macy's. Pottery Barn catalogs featuring "Madeline lamps" and "Tyler apothecary tables" matured into Williams-Sonoma catalogs featuring copper cookware and gingham table linens.

What would ultimately prove relevant in our lives were the Kmart circulars and the nameless catalogs promoting educational toys for children, both of which sent a mixed message: you are parents now, which is a blessing, but since you can no longer afford to have nice things, you might as well skim the pages of this play sand catalog. But I had stopped paying attention long before those arrived. Somewhere along the way, I had stopped paying such close attention to Kristen and her world. Because of that, our mutual world vanished. That's the egocentricity that comes with Asperger's. That's the imperceptible tide that carries people away from each other, the waters that so easily erode common ground.

Kristen and I had been working for about three months to improve communication when I decided it was time to shore up our mutual world. We needed to build a foundation from which we could reclaim our friendship, and I was determined to make it happen. It seemed like something that I had to do quietly, behind the scenes. As Kristen had explained to me dozens of times for various reasons, no sane person would ever respond favorably if told "We need to become friends, and it has to happen immediately, so let's get to work." I needed an entry point, and *Cosmo* wasn't going to cut it this time. Fortunately, we still had television.

About once a year, Kristen and I become rabidly addicted to one TV show or another. This has always been our thing. Even during the darkest period in our marriage, certain television shows reminded us that at one time we had been friends with common interests. Sometimes we wouldn't talk for days, but then *Scrubs* would come on and we'd settle onto the couch, laughing in all the same places, commenting on all the same scenes. Connecting, if only for a moment.

Some couples work out together, others read books or prepare delicious meals together. Not us. Given the opportunity, we will forever be the amorphous figures on the couch watching a fitness reality show, napping through a documentary about books, or fast-forwarding through some cooking competition on the Food Network. It's passive and mind dulling, but because we both enjoy it, television has always served as a unifying medium in our relationship.

I like to think of Kristen and myself as relatively bright people, but certain mainstays in our nightly show lineups throughout the years may prove otherwise. When we were dating, spirited conversations about *Friends* and *America's Funniest Home Videos* served my courtship well (what girl doesn't love sixty minutes of dogs on skateboards?), and our mutual love affair with *American Idol* kept us both comfortably numb amid the stress of planning our wedding. For a while, we were hooked on *Deadliest Catch,* a documentary show about crab fishermen, narrated by this absurdly dramatic voice. We liked to follow *Deadliest Catch* with a recorded episode of *The Apprentice*—the reality show starring real-estate mogul Donald Trump, which made for one fine chaser to men emptying crab pots in the rain. Before that, we were riveted by *American Chopper,* a reality show about an explosive-tempered family who all look the same and build choppers, though neither of us has any interest in motorcycles.

In the thick of a phase, the time lost on these programs wasn't measured in hours or afternoons. It was on the order of days. Especially for shows on cable networks, which tend to run weekend-long marathons. Before the kids came along, dishes would pile up in the sink—if they ever made it that far from the couch. The mailbox would become crowded with letters and magazines. The grass would grow tall and our pajamas would give in to the notion of a forty-eight-hour shift. It was awesome.

With kids in the picture now, we try not to watch so much television. When they're awake, that is. The weekend-long marathons have been supplanted by trips to the park or to the farmer's market. We let them watch one cartoon in the afternoon when we need a break, and we usually huddle together for an hour before bed to watch a family movie—Emily and Parker's reward for good behavior. But once the kids are asleep, Kristen and I convene on the couch, put our feet up, and get down to business.

Our latest obsession was a beast of a reality show called *America's Next Top Model*. Hosted by supermodel Tyra Banks, it was to Kristen and me what a warehouse of opium might be to a heroin addict. We couldn't stop watching when it was on, and we had a plan for when it wasn't. Both DVRs in the house were set to record it, and on each one we had about five hours of episodes waiting to be played, in the event that we were watching TV and it wasn't on one of the channels (which, thanks to the Oxygen network, was almost never the case). We analyzed it, asked each other questions about it, offered opinions on the fates of the contestants. I imagined other people watched news programs or police dramas that way, exchanging insightful commentary, except that we enjoyed the advantage of not having to think.

An all-girl modeling competition, the show was the couture equivalent of *American Idol,* except that one might once in a while recognize the name of an *American Idol* winner. Each week, a girl was eliminated for one reason or another: she blinked in her photographs; she displayed a poor attitude toward others; she lumbered down the runway like a yeti, one with fairer skin and high heels. I laughed and stuffed popcorn into my mouth during the teary eliminations. After a girl was chosen to go home, the screen usually flashed to a dozen clearly hotter women celebrating their successful week by running around their shared apartment in their underpants. What's not to love?

We found ourselves rooting wildly for the contestants—often for the same ones, though occasionally we didn't agree. I was incensed one week when my front-runner—a showy brunette—was eliminated. "How do you dismiss a body like that?" I protested. Kristen sided with the judges: "High fashion isn't about big boobs, Dave. These girls need an 'it' factor, which she didn't have." *Did you just say, an* "it" *factor?* It annoyed me that my expert opinion on who's hot was being challenged. When it comes to religion, politics, or finance, a ham sandwich would make a better panelist than the likes of me; I don't pay attention. But if the topic is the relative appearances of beautiful women, I suddenly have a lot to say. I become a regular James Carville. But I didn't want to argue in front of the television, and so I let it go.

In terms of entertainment value, I could have done without photo shoots and female drama. I was not interested in go-sees, and I usually couldn't discriminate between a good pose and a bad pose. What made the show so enjoyable was that I got to sit next to Kristen while we watched it. This was not at all by accident or through some proclivity to watch shows geared toward women. It was by design.

There were shows that we both enjoyed, but I tended to scoff at her while she watched certain ones—profiles of serial killers, Lifetime movies, and, at first, *America's Next Top Model*. If it didn't interest me, my reaction to it was always the same: "I can't believe you watch this garbage." She would usually get annoyed and move up to the bedroom to continue watching her show in peace, while I'd stay downstairs to find something that would suit me.

In late spring I made it a goal to knock it off. *Watch her shows and don't make fun of them,* I wrote on an envelope. There were plenty of programs to choose from, and I figured that a show about female models seemed as good a place to start as any.

Joining Kristen one evening, I sat through my first episode of *Top Model,* determined to say nothing. About halfway through, I found myself getting pulled in. "Why is that one so angry all the time?" I asked, pointing to a sourpuss contestant. "Her? Oh, she's not so bad," Kristen said. "Just catty. But she takes awesome pictures." I smiled, happy to be sharing in Kristen's moment. By the end of the episode, I was full of questions about the show: "So, what do they get if they win?" "How are they judged?" "Which girls do you like?" A few minutes later, having decided it would be easier to explain the show while it was happening, Kristen pulled up the previous week's episode. And then another. And then another. And just like that, the show became ours.

Having successfully transformed Kristen's favorite show into a portal to common ground, I began fleshing out new opportunities, more shows. Ideally, I would have created a new mutual context based on things that I enjoyed—science documentaries, Rush concert videos, anything by Monty Python or the Three Stooges. But I was enough of a realist to know that getting Kristen interested in those things was way outside the realm of possibility. I had no control over her choices, but I did have control over my own. I couldn't force her to like *South Park,* but I could choose to set down my DVD copy of *Tron* to watch a documentary about teenage ghost hunters.

Some of my friends do make fun of me for watching shows like *America's Next Top Model* and (God help me) *Project Runway.* For them, this habit is on a par with my Nora Ephron phase, that little period of time I call "1992 to present." (This has been an ongoing era for me, rich with inspiring romance, sweet comedy, and happy Hollywood endings. And yet, most of my friends would prefer to think that such a phase never existed.) They also question my enthusiasm for clothes shopping and for signing Kristen and myself up for couples' facials—this after having expanded the Best Practice to *Get inside her girl world and look around.* "Dude, that stuff is so gay," they say. *Is it?* I wonder. I cannot with any certainty give them the first and last name of any baseball player in the country, unless I've jotted it down on a flash card in an anticipatory measure taken before a big customer meeting. Kristen's just not into baseball. And yet, I have a favorite celebrity stylist—a girl named Rachel who has her own fabulous television show, which none of my gay friends seem to watch.

Whether my friends are right remains a mystery. They are often too busy watching mixed martial arts or men's professional wrestling to offer me any explanation as to why they think my interests are, as they put it, gay. For me, scantily clad female models it is. What can I say? Finding common ground in gay stuff with Kristen has led to plenty of phenomenal hetero sex for me. I guess I'd rather get some action watching *Sex and the City* than fall asleep alone on the couch with the game on.

Not that I'd have to. As if in response to my efforts, Kristen started getting into my types of shows as well. Some of them, anyway. Televised cattle auctions were pushing it, but she would cheer with me while we watched professional bull riding. "Chris Shivers just rode for eight!" she'd say. "We like him, right?" She started spending more time watching *Family Guy* and stand-up comedy specials, while I learned to sit through syndicated episodes of *Roseanne* and *Saved by the Bell.*

Our mutual world was beginning to take shape, and it felt great. Getting inside her girl world and looking around was proving to be one of my easiest Best Practices. Instead of saying, "Let's foster companionship over an awkward dinner," I was now saying, "Want to join me at the spa for my birthday?" Rather than suggesting, "Let's work on communicating tonight!" it was so much easier and more human to say, "Let's watch some TV." We'd settle in together, knowing that there would always be a big, emotional discussion waiting for us, something with no commercial interruptions or laugh tracks, and for those few hours, we'd feel as tuned-in as ever.

Chapter 4

Just listen.

Kristen and I were sitting out on our patio, enjoying a midsummer evening with a glass of wine and a cozy little fire. The leaves of our young maple trees whispered faintly overhead and broke up the bright moonlight, which glistened off our patio furniture and cast shadows from the tall wooden swing set in the corner of our lawn. While warming her toes near the fire, Kristen told me that she'd heard about a research study that was meant to determine how early in life humans can exhibit empathy.

"Apparently the researchers gathered all these infants together to see how they'd react when they heard the sound of a baby crying, and they found that if one infant cried, then most of the other infants would cry in response," she said.

I was mesmerized by the glowing embers beneath the flames in our fire pit, which made the surrounding brick come alive in a delicate, jittery light. "And?"

"Well, they think it's proof that humans can empathize when they're just a few weeks old. Isn't that amazing?"

69

I said that it was, and then I made the story about me. "I wonder if I would have cried."

We unanimously agreed that if another baby had cried, then I most certainly would have cried, too, but only because the little son of a bitch would have interrupted my sleep. What can I say? I'm just not as empathic as, well, most of the world's population. Not that it's my fault, of course.

First of all—let's face it—I'm a guy. That's strike one. To make matters worse, I'm a guy with Asperger syndrome. If empathy were currency, men with Asperger syndrome would starve. The fact that I'm also a husband basically means that if you ever want to get your feelings noticed, you pretty much have to grab me by the cheeks and say very slowly: "I. Need. You. To. Listen. To. Me." Even then, I might misinterpret your point: *Woo hoo! She's hitting me up for sex!*

With our communication skills on the mend, Kristen and I had begun talking more frequently about empathy, and more specifically my apparent deficiency in it. The topic was bound to come up; reduced empathic ability was a frustrating reality of my disorder, and by extension, our marriage. I understood that one of the major bullet points in any list of symptoms associated with autism spectrum conditions was a problematic deficiency in empathy in relation to neurotypicals. But in the first few months after my diagnosis, I wasn't certain that I had that particular symptom. *I feel stuff,* I thought.

Kristen thought differently. She was painfully aware of my deficit, having been something of a victim of my apparent insensitivity (read: cluelessness) for years. With my diagnosis, she gained a new perspective that allowed her to see that I may have been clinically self-centered, outrageously self-centered, but not *willfully* self-centered. She tried sharing this perspective with me, explaining that I hadn't been programmed for empathic ability and never would be. "And that's fine," she'd add. *Is it?* I'd wonder. *Sounds like empathy is a pretty big deal, actually.*

She began taking time to explain why certain social situations were challenging for me. Things like engaging with people in socially appropriate ways: "I think your brother really wanted to see you the other night, Dave. It's not your fault, but you missed the cues." This after my brother had offered—out of the blue—to buy me dinner one evening, and although we almost never go out together, I'd declined, saying, "I do love free food. But it's Butter Noodles Saturday, so I'm going to pass." My response had seemed perfectly acceptable to me, but to Kristen and my brother it was clear that I hadn't interpreted his emotional intent: to spend time together.

As empathy became the focus of Kristen's and my discussions, I became increasingly confused about whether or not I could empathize, and if so, how well. I couldn't begin to imagine how a person might quantify a deficit in empathy. A deficit in teeth or eyebrows would be pretty easy to assess, but what constitutes a lack of empathy?

"What if I give a shit, but just barely?" I once asked Kristen. "Would that count? What if I can determine what someone else is feeling, but I can't actually feel it myself? Or what if I could sense your sadness but never offered you any comfort? In that case, would empathy even matter? How much is 'I'm sorry' going to buy you, really? If I'm willing to be compassionate on demand, could that count for something?"

Kristen waited until I finished, then shrugged her shoulders and said, "Empathy is like talent, Dave. We're born with some amount of it, so we all function at different levels. Also, it's not a matter of 'I'm better' or 'you're worse.' We're just different."

Still, I couldn't help but feel cheated. I understood that empathy was a vital resource for successful social interactions, that it prevented one person from offending another and even drew people together, allowing them to bond in ways that are exclusive to the human experience. I felt like I was missing out on part of that experience. And looking back, I was. Engaging the social world without empathy is like going to the mall without any money or pants on; it can be done, but you're bound to have problems.

71

I didn't want to think of myself as being devoid of feeling, so I initially rejected the idea that I lacked empathy. I thought of my reactions to situations captured in films, television, and literature. I could recognize when a character offended someone important, for instance, and I would become anxious the moment he or she realized it. I understood what it meant whenever the medical director softened his eyes in a dramatic tough-love speech. I had shed tears during Folgers coffee commercials. (I didn't bother to consider the fact that had the actor in the Folgers commercial pulled me aside after the shoot and told me he had only one day left to live, I would have immediately asked him if he knew how many days I had left.)

I thought of my favorite childhood teddy bear. How I had discovered him one afternoon lying facedown on my bedroom floor and had clutched him to my chest and cried apologetically because I thought he seemed lonely. But then I thought of the countless times I'd seen my classmates burst into tears in the classroom or on the playground, and I realized that in those moments I always reacted the same way I did when I watched them take a bite out of a sandwich. *So, does the teddy bear count?* I wondered.

I also tried to convince myself that my compassion for (and understanding of) cattle counted as empathy. Growing up, we raised red Angus cattle and showed them every summer at the Illinois state and county fairs, and at my dad's comical, almost maniacal insistence, I spent a lot of time around the herd. "We're not going to half-ass this," he'd say whenever I complained. "Now get out there and brush your steer. And when you're done with that, you can wash him and brush him again." His point was that if you're going to do something, then you need to do it right. He also knew that an animal's trust is garnered over time, so I learned how to interact with our cattle, hour by hour, as the summers unfolded. Amid dusty beams of sunlight streaming in through the cracks and knotholes in the siding of the barn, I'd watch them watching me while they ate—staring with awe into the masticating faces of unimpressed cattle was an activity I found easy to focus on. Then the summer would end, and I'd be forced to sell my steer at the annual livestock auction.

I've attended funerals for loved ones where the greatest discomfort I experienced came from the suit I had to wear. But each summer, after loading my steer onto the slaughter truck, I'd suffer crying jags that would pop up randomly for days. I'd lie awake nights, thinking about him—his huge, calm, trusting eyes; his ears falling forward, relaxed; the sound of his breathing; how he just ate and looked around, totally comfortable in my presence. There was never a question in my mind as to how my steer felt in those moments I spent with him: *We have a weird relationship here, but it works. Can you do something about these flies?*

I was no expert, but to me these examples constituted some empathic ability, which made things rather confusing for me. Worse, nobody could agree on what empathy amounted to. Kristen had her definition, which differed from the one in the dictionary, which contradicted my friends' theories. And of course, none of those definitions could please the millions of contrarian bloggers I found when I searched for the term online—faceless people with names like CaptainHamwhistle who stay up nights rethinking their avatars and who themselves couldn't define the concept yet insisted that any mainstream definition was not to be trusted.

With no clear definition of empathy, and no way of quantifying how much of it I had or didn't have, I resorted to actual research to get to the bottom of things. I sequestered myself in Kristen's office one evening while she was watching a movie—some tearjerker I had no business getting myself involved in. *Beaches,* I think it was. My first Internet search included the keywords *empathy, Asperger,* and *syndrome,* and the results were rather useless—confusing wiki threads, links to videos of purportedly clairvoyant house cats, that sort of thing. Then I added the word *measuring* to my search parameters, and within minutes I had all the answers I needed.

There were many results to choose from, but I started with an article titled "The Empathy Quotient: An Investigation of Adults with Asperger Syndrome," which had been written by Simon Baron-Cohen and Sally Wheelwright of the Autism Research Centre at the University of Cambridge. (Leave it to renowned experts and leading researchers to really know what they're talking about. No offense, CaptainHamwhistle.)

In the article, Baron-Cohen and Wheelwright spelled out in no uncertain terms—and I'm paraphrasing here—that my wife had been right all along. I do in fact have a measurable deficiency in empathic ability. My Empathy Quotient? Using Baron-Cohen's method, I earned a meager fifteen points out of a possible eighty. That's 19 percent. Talk about just barely giving a shit. The study's control group—neurotypicals—averaged in the forties. (Interestingly, a second study revealed that among the general population, women scored significantly higher than men. A point that will come as no surprise to women.)

According to Baron-Cohen and Wheelwright, empathy is "the drive or ability to attribute mental states to another person/animal, and entails an appropriate affective response in the observer to the other person's mental state." *Hmm.* I called up the stairs to Kristen, asking her what *affective* meant.

"Affective what?" she asked.

"I don't know. Just affective."

"Relating to an emotional state," she called.

Oh. Okay, this makes sense. I wrote the definition down in my notebook. *So* this *is what I'm lacking!*

Baron-Cohen's first article inspired me to read more. In all the subsequent searches I made sure to include his name, and by the end of the evening I had a stack of clinical papers on the subject. I had empirical data rather than conjecture, which meant that I finally had answers.

What I gleaned from all this research is that empathy is the result of numerous cognitive and affective processes, all firing away behind the scenes somewhere in our brains. Cognitive processes allow us to understand the mental state of another person—his or her emotions, desires, beliefs, intentions, et cetera—which in turn helps us to understand and even predict the person's actions or behaviors. They allow us to step outside of our own experience in order to take on and understand other people's perspectives—something that every wife on the planet wishes her husband would do. The affective component of empathy is more related to our emotional responses to the mental states that we observe in other people. This component allows us to *feel* some appropriate and non-egocentric emotional response to another person's emotions—something *else* that every wife on the planet wishes her husband would do.

Empathy involves both processes, and while they operate independently of one another, there is some overlap. A graphical representation of empathy might involve a Venn diagram—two circles, one for the affective component and one for the cognitive, slightly overlapping, with me standing well outside of both circles talking incessantly about the weather during a funeral.

In people with Asperger syndrome and other autism spectrum conditions, these mechanisms of understanding are much less reliable and productive than in neurotypicals. Those of us living within the parameters of an autism spectrum condition simply can't engage the empathic processes that allow for social reasoning and emotional awareness. Furthermore, we have difficulty separating ourselves from our own perspectives (the word *autism* comes from the Greek word *autos,* meaning "self"), so we can't easily understand or even access the perspectives and feelings of others.

This explains why I sat in bird poo in junior high school, to the profound amusement of popular kids. Had I access to the appropriate cognitive resources, I might have been able to recognize the motivations of the douchebags who had insisted that I sit with them, "in that spot, right there." I thought they actually wanted me to join them, even though they couldn't remember my name or keep themselves from laughing.

Reduced empathic ability also partially accounts for my gross misinterpretation of social exchanges. I wrongly estimate the intentions that underlie the interaction, and in so doing, I make a fool of myself. Kristen and I might meet a couple at a party, and if I feel any sort of connection with them, I'll pull Kristen aside and start hounding her: "We need to become close friends with these people as soon as possible. Invite them over this weekend. They like us, it's obvious. He mentioned they have a boat—that was an invitation for us to join them on it, right?"

"They were just talking to us the way people do at parties," Kristen will say, looking at me skeptically. "I think they might be drunk."

On the way home, we might argue about it. I will insist that Kristen just blew the friendship opportunity of a lifetime, and she will maintain her position that it's creepy to tell strangers that you'd like to become close friends with them, adding, "And you should never say 'as soon as possible.'"

Whenever I find myself sitting in bird poo or demanding close relationships from complete strangers, I can chalk it up to God-given faulty cognitive processes. To me, this is great news. I don't have to be embarrassed anymore about my social cluelessness. I can't be expected to predict the intentions of others and assume their perspectives any more than I can be expected to rebuild a carburetor or sit down at a piano to knock out a Rachmaninoff concerto; I wasn't born with that particular talent.

The not-so-great news is that my affective (emotional) responses are also reduced, a phenomenon that severely undermines my abilities as a husband. Embarrassing myself at a cocktail party is one thing. Not being able to recognize when Kristen needs my support is something else entirely.

After Emily was born, Kristen struggled with postpartum depression. We didn't recognize it at first. Something wasn't right, she wasn't herself, but we assumed that her moods and exhaustion were due only to the surprising demands of being a first-time mom.

Kristen had dreamed of having children since she was herself a child and had always thought that she would love motherhood as much as she would love her babies. "I know that being a mom will be demanding," she told me once. "But I don't think it will change me much. I'll still have my life, and our baby will be part of it." She envisioned long walks through the neighborhood with Emily. She envisioned herself mastering the endlessly repeating three-hour cycle of playing, feeding, sleeping, and diaper changing. Most of all, she envisioned a full parenting partnership, in which I'd help whenever I was home—morning, nighttime, and weekends. Of course, I didn't know any of this until she told me, which she did after Emily was born.

At first, the newness of parenthood made it seem as though everything was going according to our expectations. *We'll be up all day and all night for a few weeks, but then we'll hit our stride and our lives will go back to normal, plus one baby.* Kristen took a few months off from work to focus all of her attention on Emily, knowing that it would be hard to juggle the contradicting demands of an infant and a career. She was determined to own motherhood. "We're still in that tough transition," Kristen would tell me, trying to console Emily at four A.M. "Pretty soon, we'll find our routine. I hope."

But things didn't go as we had planned. There were complications with breast-feeding. Emily wasn't gaining weight; she wouldn't eat, wouldn't sleep, wouldn't play. She was born in December, when it was far too cold to go for walks outdoors. While I was at work, Kristen would sit on the floor with Emily in the dark—all the lights off, all the shades closed—and cry. She'd think about her friends, all of whom had made motherhood look so easy with their own babies. "Mary had no problem breast-feeding," she'd tell me. "Jenny said that these first few months had been her favorite. Why can't I get the hang of this?" I didn't have any answers, but still I offered solutions, none of which she wanted to hear: "Talk to a lactation consultant about the feeding issues." "Establish a routine and stick to it." Eventually, she stopped talking altogether.

While Kristen struggled, I watched from the sidelines, unaware that she needed help. I excused myself from the nighttime and morning responsibilities, as the interruptions to my daily schedule became too much for me to handle. We didn't know this was because of a developmental disorder; I just looked incredibly selfish. I contributed, but not fully. I'd return from work, and Kristen would go upstairs to sleep for a few hours while I'd carry Emily from room to room, gently bouncing her as I walked, trying to keep her from crying. But eventually eleven o'clock would roll around and I'd go to bed, and Kristen would be awake the rest of the night with her. The next morning, I would wake up and leave for work, while Kristen stared down the barrel of another day alone.

To my surprise, I grew increasingly disappointed in her: *She wanted to have children. Why is she miserable all the time? What's her problem?* I also resented what I had come to recognize as our failing marriage. I'd expected our marriage to be happy, fulfilling, overflowing with constant affection. My wife was supposed to be able to handle things like motherhood with aplomb. Kristen loved me, and she loved Emily, but that wasn't enough for me. In my version of a happy marriage, my wife would also love the difficulties of *being* my wife and *being* a mom. It hadn't occurred to me that I'd have to earn the happiness, the fulfillment, the affection. Nor had it occurred to me that she might have her own perspective on marriage and motherhood.

Spring finally arrived, and Kristen started taking Emily out for walks. The sunshine illuminated something important for her—it wasn't normal to sit in the dark and cry all day. She brought this up one afternoon while we were out for a walk together with Emily. "That's all I do," she said. "I sing to her, I play with her, and I cry. I never feel like getting dressed, I never feel like doing anything. Ever." We walked a few blocks in silence before I said that it seemed she hadn't been herself in months. Sobbing, she admitted that she felt the same way. We had been living with her symptoms but had misidentified their source. It was not unlike the discovery that I was an undiagnosed Aspie.

Kristen eventually sought treatment and started taking medication for her depression, and she bounced back almost immediately. It was a relief to see her come back so quickly. It was a relief to see her come back, period. She felt better, but her medication couldn't alleviate her resentment toward me for not displaying even a shred of empathy during that period of loneliness. I showed compassion at times, and I showed concern. But neither of those are empathy.

"You got your life back the moment you returned to work," she often told me. "This is so hard for me, and you just don't get that."

I would respond the only way I knew how—egocentrically and analytically: "My job pays for everything and gives us health insurance. I have to work, Kristen. Never mind that I hate my job, and that it makes me miserable, and then I come home to total anguish. My life's hard, too."

Responses like that did a lot of damage, as did my subsequent attempts at guidance: "So, if this is all too much for you, then let's figure something out. Let's schedule our days so we can be sure you're getting a break when you need one."

She tried (God, how she tried) to explain that she wasn't looking for solutions. She wasn't looking for sob stories about my job. All she was looking for was this: "Mmm-hmm. I totally hear you." That's all.

"Emily wouldn't sleep today? Mmm-hmm. I totally hear you. That must have been rough."

"You're mad because I got to go golfing with customers today and we had sushi for lunch? Mmm-hmm. I totally see your point. It's not fair that I get to do those things and you don't."

"You need a few minutes to yourself when I get home? Mmm-hmm. I get it. You must be exhausted."

It should have been that simple. She didn't need me to fix anything for her (but when she did, she knew how to ask). She didn't need me to coddle her. She just needed me to listen and appreciate her situation. But you couldn't tell me that back then. Not without a few hours of analytical follow-up discussion.

Everything changed when we discovered that I have Asperger syndrome. My diagnosis gave Kristen a new perspective on things. Finding it too painful to concede that her husband wasn't willing to put himself in her shoes, she instead put her faith in the bullet point: because of his syndrome, my husband isn't *able* to put himself in my shoes. This made things much more bearable for her. Dave doesn't understand my feelings . . . because his brain can't process them. Dave didn't put my needs above his own . . . because he didn't see I was depressed. Dave makes hurtful comments about my abilities as a mom . . . because he doesn't understand how difficult motherhood is.

Prior to my diagnosis, Kristen often told me in frustration, "You *just don't* GET IT, Dave." Now that we know I have Asperger's, Kristen still finds herself saying those exact words all the time. The difference is that she now says them calmly, as a matter of fact. "You just don't get it, Dave. Your brain doesn't work that way."

A diagnosis is not a cure, of course. It's a starting point. My hope was that I could hone some of the cognitive processes associated with empathy, such as perspective switching and behavior prediction, as a skill of sorts, and find other ways to compensate for the lack of affective prowess. Things like keeping a Journal of Best Practices.

Kristen believed that I could cultivate certain social skills that would pass for empathy in a pinch, and I was excited when she agreed to work with me to develop them. She suggested that we start with listening skills. "You're doing awesome with the talking," she told me one morning as we were cleaning up the kids' breakfasts, which were all over the kitchen floor. "But sometimes, all I need is for you to listen. Let me vent so I can feel better." I tore a page out of the *New Yorker* that was sitting on our countertop, grabbed a pen, and scribbled down *Empathy—sometimes she just needs you to listen.* I said that seemed easy enough and asked what else we could work on, and she smiled. "Let's just get you listening. I think that's enough for now."

With Kristen's help, I dabbled for a few months in the art of listening. She had been right—it wasn't easy. My natural tendencies were hard to overcome. Kristen would start talking about frustrations at her job, and I'd interrupt her with unsolicited practical advice. She would stare blankly into her day planner and mention, as if to herself, "I just don't know when to schedule this new kid on my caseload." I'd get involved, saying something like, "How many kids do you see on Wednesdays? Where are they located? I can help you make a spread-sheet that includes travel times and then we can pinpoint the optimal time slot for him." Other times, she made not-so-subtle hints asking for help, which I blew off. "Ugh!" she'd growl, tripping over a tower of wooden blocks. "This toy room is a mess!" I'd stand next to her, nodding: "Mmm-hmm. I know what you mean." Then I'd go watch TV, leaving her to deal with the cleanup.

The misinterpretations of Kristen's needs were nonstop, as were my attempts at drawing out relevant discussions. Her shoes were kind of hurting her toes; she wished she knew how batteries worked; she was feeling a little groggy lately. These situations didn't require immediate action or extended dialogue. Just a nod. But how was I to know? Never mind the fact that I had just mastered talking again; around Kristen, I was like a golden retriever who had suddenly learned how to speak

English. I had so much to say about every topic. "Tell me more about your paper cut! I'll heat up some coffee!"

We inevitably argued as frustration over the process and over my shortcomings manifested itself. "There's nothing to sort out, Dave," she'd say, rolling her eyes. "I was just mentioning that my normal route to work was slow today." And I'd wonder, *If you didn't want to hammer out a solution, then why did you bring it up?*

Frustration was to be expected. Like a wobbly, newborn fawn, I was having trouble getting on my feet. It might have been cute the first few times I messed up, but we'd been at it for a couple of months and I was starting to get upset by my lack of progress. *Screw this empathy.* But Kristen kept encouraging me. "You have to remember that your brain doesn't process this naturally. This may never come easily for you, but you're doing great."

That autumn, Kristen's dad, Jim, became seriously ill and was hospitalized for two weeks. Because her parents are divorced, and because she is their only child, the responsibility of Jim's care fell entirely on Kristen. I've heard of other people our age flying across the country to take care of their parents after they had fallen ill. Some had considered the geographical divide a reasonable excuse to leave after a few days, while others had made longer-term arrangements. We didn't have to worry about that. Jim happened to live only a few miles away from us.

The first few days Jim was in the hospital were chaotic, and I did my best to be supportive while I silently obsessed over the notion of how this hospitalization might interrupt my week. (*Silently,* meaning it was something of a personal accomplishment not to have mentioned it.) Kristen needed to be at the hospital all day, so I stayed home with the kids. It was just as well that I did—I'm pretty useless in hospitals because I am absolutely terrified of them. The few times I visited Jim

I was pale and sweaty and nurses were constantly asking if I needed to lie down. Upon entering his room, I was always told to have a seat. *But where? The sickest people within a hundred miles of my house are right here in this building, and probably half of them have sat in that chair.* I touched nothing, said nothing—just stared at my feet, pressing my fingertips to my face to make sure I was still conscious. Nurses greeted me with a pat on the back—"And this greenish-looking fellow must be Kristen's husband! Heard a lot about you!" *Oh, lord. Please don't touch me.*

Kristen, in her usual way, handled things much better than I did. She'd kick back and lounge in a soft hospital chair, putting her feet up on her dad's bed. She'd watch television, read magazines, or talk to other patients while her dad slept. Sometimes, under protest from me, she would wake Jim up to let him know I was there. He'd ask how I was doing, he'd joke about the hospital food, and I would offer monosyllabic responses, aware that my breathing was shallow and frantic—aware that I could die at any second. *How could he do this to me?* Kristen would grab me by the hand and try her best to keep the conversation going, knowing how much her dad loved to talk to me.

We made it through the first week without much difficulty, but things started to unravel the following week. The specialist hadn't shown up for a few days, the neurologist wasn't being responsive to Kristen's concerns, and the insurance people were making things impossibly—almost artfully—difficult. Kristen's spirit was waning and instead of listening I tried rolling up my sleeves and fixing everything for her.

"Venting solves nothing," I told her one evening. "We need to track down this specialist and confront him. We need to find an advocate who will help us with the insurance stuff. And if the neurologist is blowing you off, then I'll go stand in front of him until he agrees to listen to you."

"Dave, forget it. I can handle this. I just wanted to talk."

"So, let's talk. Let's put a game plan together."

She looked at me for a second or two, then said, "Forget it. I'm tired," and went to bed.

I spent the rest of the evening sitting at the kitchen table with my notebook, writing about what had happened to see if I could determine where I'd gone wrong. What may have been plainly obvious to someone else had left me confounded—I simply couldn't interpret her reaction. I replayed the exchange countless times in my head and got nowhere. Finally, I wrote down, *Just be there for her.* I was still stumped as to how, so I packed up and called it a night.

The next day, I let the kids enjoy an all-day cartoons marathon. I was lying with them on the couch, still in my pajamas, staring at the ceiling and devising a strategy for Jim's care, when Kristen called. Her voice sounded small and shaky. Defeated.

"Can you come and get me?" she asked.

"Sure. What about the kids?"

"My mom's on her way over to watch them. I just . . ." She paused and sighed as if the air were too heavy to hold. "When she gets there, just come over. Please."

When I arrived at the hospital, Kristen was outside, waiting. Her face looked strained, as though she were bracing herself against the cold wind. I kept telling myself to simply be there for her, whatever that meant. I wanted to do this right.

Sliding into the front seat of my car, Kristen sniffled, and I could see that she was fighting back tears. I put my hand on her leg and asked if she was okay, and she nodded. "Just drive somewhere," she said. I shifted my car into drive and began circling the parking lot, slowly and awkwardly. *Has she snapped? Does she want food? Does she want to hear some music?* On our third time around, she asked me what I was doing, and I admitted that I didn't know and was afraid to ask. "Just go somewhere," she said. "But not here."

I was pulling onto the highway when Kristen finally made it clear how I needed to help her. "Okay," she said, trying to sound patient, as if it were perfectly normal to have to tell her husband how to engage with her. "I need to talk, and I just need you to listen to me. You may not interrupt me, you may not offer to fix anything for me, you may not give me any advice, and you may not act like you're as mad as I am. Okay? I just need you to listen."

"Okay." *Just drive and listen.* It was a test, and with things having been spelled out so clearly, I finally felt ready for it.

For ten minutes, Kristen unloaded. As she slashed her way through her anger and frustration, I went into hyper-stifling mode, indicating that I was listening by nodding my head and offering single-word responses instead of what was on my mind:

". . . He can hardly walk to the bathroom . . ."

"Mmm-hmm." *You really should eat something—your body needs nutrition.*

". . . And then this new doctor who I've never seen before comes in and starts talking about discharging Dad . . ."

"Okay." *I hope you can get home early tonight. Emily's been sad at bedtime without you.*

". . . And he is obviously freezing in there this morning, and nobody brought him a blanket . . ."

"Man." *What?! Those bastards. Give me two minutes in front of that charge nurse and I swear to God, your dad will be swimming in blankets.*

We were making a U-turn by a cleared soybean field outside of town when I realized that for the past ten minutes, I hadn't been making things harder for Kristen. Instead, I had been listening and it had felt *good.* It was a victory for me, and for Kristen, who had finally found the way to get through to me: directness. It wasn't exactly empathy, and it wasn't exactly romantic, but it worked. I wanted to ask her for a high five, but it seemed an odd thing to ask of someone whose father was hooked up to machines, so instead I did my best to expand our moment of success. "Right." "Yep." "I understand."

Later that evening, I sat down in the family room with my notebook and logged our first real victory in what I hoped would become a successful path to empathy, or something like it. *Sometimes, she just needs you to listen.* I was scribbling some thoughts about the difficulty in knowing when and how to listen, and how I needed Kristen to tell me what she needed from me, when she came downstairs in her pajamas and joined me. "Hi, hang on," I said.

She sat patiently on the couch until I finished, and when I closed my notebook, she said the most amazing thing I'd heard in months: "I know today wasn't easy for you, but that drive was exactly what I needed. It made all the difference in the world to me. Thank you so much."

Yes.

I wanted to talk about our win. I wanted her to read my journal entry. But I didn't want to blow the progress I'd just made, so I kept my response short: "I'm glad it helped. I want to be there for you." *Today I felt a little more like the husband I want to be for you. I mean, who knows? Maybe over time, this will even become my typical way of behaving! Wouldn't that be great? I can totally see myself being Mr. Empathy!* "I love you," I added.

"I love you, too."

She kissed me good night and had made it halfway up the stairs before I finally burst.

"Hey, today was really exciting for me." She stopped, and I got up from the couch to continue: "I mean, I know this week isn't about me, and I should probably not talk right now, but I've been going nuts trying to develop this empathy. I know I wasn't quite empathic this afternoon, but it did feel good to give you what you needed, even if you had to ask for it."

"It felt good for me, too." She yawned.

"Just think. If I can talk *and* listen, and somehow do it all without being selfish, then I'll pretty much be the total package. Right?"

She continued up the steps, laughing. "That's right. A selfless man who knows when to listen. I don't know what more a woman could ask for."

I honestly don't know, either. Seriously. What else could there be?

Chapter 5

Laundry: Better to fold and put away than to take only what you need from the dryer.

*L*AUNDRY. Late one night I wrote the word in large, sloppy capitals in my journal, then underlined it twice. Beside it, I wrote: *Better to fold and put away than to take only what you need from the dryer.*

This was clearly going to be my next Best Practice. It had been a long time coming, and I was none too thrilled. Rekindling the spirit of our friendship, talking about things that bothered me, listening to the things that bothered Kristen—these Best Practices were romantic and intimate, and committing myself to them every morning had made me feel redeemed and somewhat heroic. But folding laundry? *Come on.*

The evening started off casually enough. Kristen and I had gotten the kids to bed, and we were standing in the kitchen, eating M&M's. The clock on the oven read 8:37. We had the whole night ahead of us.

"What do you want to do?" Kristen asked, leaning into me for a hug.

I slid my hands down the back of her pants and took a minute to mull it over. Then another minute. And another, before she caught on and got annoyed.

We, of course, ended up on the couch, watching a movie. Kristen had done some laundry earlier in the day, and after taking our seats, we found ourselves fenced in by several stacks of loosely folded clothes. A tower of underpants nearly collapsed into my popcorn bowl, so I moved the clothes to the opposite end of the couch; Kristen muttered something and relocated them to the coffee table. I wondered— silently—why she didn't take the clothes upstairs and put them away. After all, she had separated them, washed and dried them, and folded them. Why not just put in that little extra effort to finish the job? I chewed it over as I pulled the lever to raise my footrest and recline my section of the sofa. *I mean, really, what is it with her?*

"I wonder if we could commit to being tidy," I said. "You know, to follow through on chores."

"Follow through on what chores?" Kristen asked.

Gesturing toward the stacks of clothes on the coffee table, I began digging my own grave: "Putting things away, for instance."

"Oh-ho-ho," she said, "that's a great idea, Dave. Be my guest." She grabbed the remote control off my chest and paused the movie. "Go ahead. Take the clothes upstairs and put them away. That would be a great start. Thank you so much. I'll keep the movie paused."

"What, are you mad at me?"

"No, I'm not mad at all. Come on. Hurry up, so we can finish the movie." Her voice didn't sound mad. Her face didn't look mad. But she sure seemed mad. Even with my rudimentary empathy skills I could see it.

"I'll just take them upstairs when we go to bed," I offered, shoving more popcorn into my mouth. "We don't have to do it right now."

"Are you kidding?" Kristen asked. Now she did look mad. "Do you know how long those clothes sat in the damn dryer?"

"A few days," I said.

"Right. A few days. And instead of taking everything out, folding it, and putting it away, you're in there every morning for ten minutes, picking through the entire load for the one thing you need."

Kristen was right. I'm not the sort of person who sees clothes in the dryer and takes action. Partly because when it's time for me to get dressed, I know exactly what I need. The gray boxers. The large white T-shirt. The narrow-ribbed black socks. If they aren't in my drawer, then I head to the laundry room. *Ah, there they are.* If they are unfolded, it makes no difference. I just root through the dryer until I find whatever it is I'm looking for. To make things easier on everyone else, I choose to leave the pile in the dryer if possible, which seems preferable to leaving clothes out where people have to sit. I rarely receive gratitude for this measure of consideration.

"When am I supposed to have time to fold clothes?" I asked. "Find the time in my day to fold laundry. Is it when I'm getting ready for work? Is it when I'm at work? Is it when I'm driving home from work? Playing with the kids? Cleaning up the kitchen? Would that be a good time for me to fold laundry?" I was being snotty because she was 100 percent right, and I felt cornered. So of course, I made no mention of the amount of time that I spend in the bathroom, or the two hours that I spend getting ready in the morning before leaving for work, or the blocks of time that I devote to staring out our front windows, internally reciting first and last names. These appropriations of time were totally irrelevant to this conversation, as far as I was concerned.

"Give it a rest, Dave. I'm sure that once in a while you can find ten minutes in your version of a twenty-four-hour day to empty the dryer," she said. "Or to take laundry that I've *already folded* out of the laundry room and bring it upstairs. That's all I'm asking."

Kristen had a good point, but I wasn't interested in acknowledging it yet, so I said nothing. She resumed the movie, adding, "It would be nice if you were as obsessed with doing laundry as you are with your bathroom habits."

Crap. Another good point. If laundry were one of my special habits, then I would stop at nothing to ensure that it was done properly: every article would be separated, washed, dried, folded neatly, and put away in its rightful place. Completing the job any other way might cause my head to explode. Much to Kristen's disappointment, however, the process of doing laundry isn't something with which I've ever been obsessed. Clean clothes, yes. Correctly folded clothes, absolutely. If the alternative is incorrectly folded clothes, I'd rather they remain unfolded. As for caring about whether they're lying in drawers or in piles around the house, I have my preferences, but they're not so strong that I'm motivated to do anything about them.

Laundry isn't the only household task that hasn't made my list of essentials. Getting the mail, making the beds, tidying up—these activities are all up for grabs. That's the double-edged nature of my obsessive mind. When it works in my favor, obsession leads to great accomplishments. Free from normal human distractions like opening mail or accommodating the needs of others, I am able to put all of my mental energy into achieving goals that are intrinsically important to me—closing a deal to boost my career or modifying personal behaviors to repair relationships. But obsession can work against me. Certain interests can distract me from successful engagement in useful endeavors. I am likely to focus on perfecting the bawl of a nervous cow, or juggling, rather than mowing the lawn and interacting with my children, respectively. If I don't obsess about something then it doesn't get done.

Unfortunately, I'm not always able to pick my obsessions, as anyone who has ever ridden in my car will attest. "Hold on," I say to passengers as we approach the car. "I'm very sorry, just let me move some things to make room . . ."

He or she will wait patiently, and I'll sense their eagerness to comment on what would astound anyone: stacks of loose papers with notes, thoughts, and diagrams scribbled across them. Countless unopened envelopes—bills, second, third, and final notices, many of which have also been marked with notes, thoughts, and diagrams. Bowls and plates sprinkled with pepper granules and bread crumbs are stacked five to ten high or scattered across the front passenger floor. Cups with dried orange juice or old tea caked to the bottom are strewn about. CDs run wild and garbage-stuffed Burger King bags serve as a sort of mound on which the passenger may rest his or her elbow.

After I've made enough room on one seat or another for the person to sit down and buckle in, I usually hear something like "Wow. You seem so freaked out about everything else, I'm really surprised by how filthy this car is." *Yup*.

While we're driving, the passengers like to blather on and on about God knows what, unaware that I'm busy grouping and transforming numbers on license plates into letters in order to see which words I can spell. Then they are always surprised to hear the same Peter Gabriel songs playing over and over and over. This, to me, is incredibly amusing. "Funny," they say, "'Secret World' was playing in your car the last time you picked me up." I don't offer an explanation. I'm too busy timing the blinks of my eyes to when my car's hood is positioned precisely between two lane lines.

Of course, I'm not the only person, Aspie or neurotypical, with a preoccupied mind or a messy car. I don't know very many people who open the mail the moment it arrives. The difference is how extreme the preoccupations are for me and the extent to which the associated hang-ups affect me and my family. Most people can have something on their minds without ignoring their families or the world around them. But my brain doesn't work that way. If I were to stop indulging my obsessions, then my life would be nothing but stress. An odd but analogous situation might involve a person in a full-body cast filled with mosquitoes—all itch and no scratch. All stress and no relief. Completing certain chores doesn't give me a sense of fulfillment toward an obsession. It doesn't scratch the itch. So rather than doing them, I engage in activities that do offer relief and pacify my mind: taking lengthy showers, for example, or forcing Kristen into discussions about whether she likes spending time with me.

Fortunately for me and my family, with a lot of discipline and some strategic reprogramming of my brain, I could learn how to manage my obsessions. Transformation is always an option. I simply had to learn how to defer my engagement with a special activity and how to indulge an obsession without overindulging. I had to learn how to respond to the demands of real life without coming unglued.

With Kristen's help, I had already made some progress in this area during the months that followed my diagnosis. Kristen knew right away that I needed to be shown how to manage myself, so at first she was firm and spelled things out for me as clearly as possible: "Parker just wants you to play trains with him, Dave. You can't make him wait for an hour while you 'optimize the configuration of the tracks.'" I'd note her advice in my Journal of Best Practices and try not to repeat my mistakes.

By summer, we were picking our battles together; if I felt strongly about watching the first few minutes of *Live with Regis and Kelly* uninterrupted, then I'd lock myself in our bedroom and watch until the segment was over while Kristen sat downstairs with the kids. By fall, I had learned that I could simply force myself out of certain habits, irrespective of how critical the habit might seem: *My children are downstairs screaming; maybe I don't have to review the symmetry of my face right now.* So I'd step away from the mirror, making a mental note that the sky had not fallen in as a result of doing so. Then I'd go downstairs to tend to the kids before logging the moment as a success. *So* this *is what neurotypicals are up to. Crazy.*

Managing obsessive behaviors was one thing; convincing myself to become obsessed with laundry to ensure that it would get done would have been something else entirely. That's not to say that it would have been impossible. Kristen and I had made cleaning the kitchen one of my special interests, but that was something that sort of evolved. In 2006, about two years before I was diagnosed, I had started an argument not unlike our discussion of laundry. My point had been that I expected Kristen to keep the kitchen clean at all times. "You're here all day with Emily anyway," I said. "It'll give you something to do." (Sometimes I use words, but I choose them very poorly.) Her counterpoint involved the F-word, and the next day, I became permanently responsible for keeping the kitchen clean. "As clean as you want to make it, dear," she specified. For over two years, I honored my responsibility under severe protest. *This is bullshit. I hate this.* But in 2008, with my commitment to restoring our marriage came a new philosophy: *Do this one daily chore for your family, and don't be miserable while you do it.*

The inspiration seemed to come from nowhere, although it's possible that I was just trying to score that day—proof that necessity is the mother of invention. In any case, I gave it a shot one evening. *Just clean up and be happy about it. See how she reacts.* I expected Kristen to laud my cheery disposition and was surprised when she didn't seem to notice it. I would have accepted a standing ovation or even a cookie for my efforts, but Kristen's reward system is far more subtle. Cuddled up together later that evening, I realized my reward was the absence of resentment, and after she fell asleep, I logged the lesson in my journal: *Harboring resentment is more fatiguing and less rewarding than simply completing the task. Plus, she seems to like being around you more when you're not miserable.*

The more I practiced cleaning the kitchen without being angry, the easier and more natural it became. I'd begin clearing the table, and an hour later (I never said I could do it quickly), I would have a perfectly spotless kitchen in which I could pace around and clear my head, and my great mood would make Kristen want to spend time with me, which was what I wanted more than anything.

But the question remained: If this sense of discipline is possible, then why can't I just fold that frigging laundry?

This is the question that Kristen finds herself asking, albeit in different forms on different days. *If he can arrange our mail by envelope*

*width, why can't he just open it? If he can spend ten minutes relacing his
shoes so that the strings are of perfectly equal length, why can't he just put
them in the closet when he takes them off? If he can call me on my way to
work to ask if I'd planned to make the bed, why couldn't he have just made
it himself?* When Kristen enters the kitchen and finds me still cleaning
an hour after I've started, the answer is clearly revealed: I tend to com-
plicate things.

"Are you still cleaning?" she'll ask. Prior to my diagnosis, I would
hear this question as "Why is this taking you so long? Why are you
so stupid? Someday I will leave you because of this." I would go nuts,
throwing my hands into the air like a maniac and barking back, "I'm
sorry that what I'm doing still isn't good enough for you, sweetheart.
How's this?" Then, in an immediate and dizzying rage, I'd slam every
dirty dish straight into the dishwasher, some of them missing completely and crashing to the floor, while she stormed out of the room,
saying into the air, "I am so . . . fucking . . . *done* with this shit."

Now, though, having come a long way in our communication,
I take the question for what it really is: natural curiosity about a process—a process that, I like to think, is the product of genius. I understand that she's surprised, as anybody would be, by how long it takes
me to clear a few dishes and wipe down the counter. I usually respond
with a nod, if I can pull myself away from my focused cleaning efforts
long enough to do so.

Sometimes she'll come over and give me a hug, and as I freeze in
place to accept her affection, I can feel her observing my operation.
First, it's all dishes into the sink, carried one by one from the table
and inspected for remnants. Then they are separated by group: plates
and bowls in the left basin; glasses, cups, silverware, and utensils in
the right. All silverware is then inserted into a single glass, which is
filled with water (I call this "presoaking"). Next, the bowls and plates
are hand-scrubbed one at a time and deposited into the dishwasher,
followed by glasses and silverware. Loading the dishwasher takes me

a while—it's an iterative loop designed for ease of unloading, the goal being to arrange the plates and bowls just as they are grouped in our cupboard: dinner plates, salad plates, soup bowls. Glasses and silverware are subjected to the same organization. All this effort pays off when I unload; I can simply grab entire groups of dishes and place them in the cupboard.

When Kristen loads the dishwasher, the process is far less optimized—it doesn't matter to her if plates and pots share a row or if bowls mingle with glasses. I find myself having to put dishes away one at a time, rather than in clusters, which is so tedious, frustrating, and unnecessary that my head begins to hurt and I find myself questioning her thought processes, if not her motives. *Forks and spoons bundled together? Is she trying to kill me?*

After I finish the dishes, the counter gets wiped down, as do the chairs and the table. I leave the cooktop alone most nights because the first minute spent cleaning a cooktop inevitably leads to fifteen more. I wash the sink, line the toaster up parallel to the edge of the counter, wash my hands, and—sixty minutes after I've started—I call it a night.

Folding clothes presents a similar set of challenges. Whereas Kristen can fold a shirt, then a pair of boxers, then a towel, and stack them all together while watching TV or talking, I am forced by my own logic to take a different approach.

Again my objective is the most sensible strategy for putting things away, so I stack everything in groups: boxers, T-shirts, pajamas. Because stacks are involved, they must be straight, requiring each fold to be precise and creased hard, like a paper airplane. I can't have any distractions, and still a basket might take half an hour to fold, or longer if, heaven help me, socks are in the mix. (I only purchase one style of white sock, so those are easy. It's the dress socks that need special attention—they're all such little individuals.)

Folding takes me forever, so I just don't do it. Kristen does, and I'm always hesitant to inform her that she does it incorrectly. Due perhaps to carelessness, her hectic work schedule, or the fact that two children and a fully grown husband are constantly hanging off her and begging for attention, Kristen's method is much more haphazard—there's no telling how the boxers might be folded, and my T-shirts are always folded in on themselves, making it impossible to determine the color of the size label located just below the collar without unfolding the whole thing. This is a problem, as I've reserved shirts with red labels for casual dress and those with black labels for important occasions. *Is she kidding?* I'll wonder as I unroll a white T-shirt. *Who folds shirts like this? It would have been easier to pick through the dryer.*

I always have the option of unfolding all my shirts and refolding them, so long as I accomplish it in such a way that Kristen never, ever, ever finds out, because if she did, nothing of mine would ever be folded by her hands again. And sometimes, locked inside our bedroom closet after she's gone to work, I do.

Kristen has often suggested that I try a little *less* when I set out to accomplish something, that perhaps it would make things easier on me. But that philosophy doesn't compute at all. Everything I want to accomplish is done with the precision of a military operation. It's exhausting, but it's the only way for me. This is where Kristen and I differ. To me, a task is a puzzle comprised of a million tiny pieces that must be arranged properly. Usually I find myself more appreciative of the procedure than of the outcome itself. Kristen, on the other hand, sees the process only as the means to an end. I see the trees, in other words, and Kristen sees the forest. Or, more to the point, I see a handsome genius declining involvement in an excruciating process, while Kristen sees a fully grown, half-naked man, covered in a towel, rummaging through a major home appliance for a pair of underpants.

We were midway through our movie, and the laundry had yet to be put away. Kristen appeared to be enjoying the film, but I was busy ruminating and had tuned it out completely. I was trying to find some insight into my laundry aversion so that we could discuss it further. I knew that folding wasn't an obsession of mine. I knew that I would make the process painfully difficult for myself. But I also knew that those obstacles could be overcome with willpower. The biggest challenge was this: I couldn't shake the feeling that I shouldn't have been the one doing laundry in the first place. *That's her job.* This was not the sort of thing a guy could safely announce to his wife, especially during a Hugh Grant movie, but it felt like such a significant factor. I should have let the matter go, but instead I kept digging.

"I'd like to blame this on my parents," I said.

"What? What are you talking about?" Kristen paused the movie, and now I had Hugh Grant grinning at me from inside my television, as if he were thinking, *Right, now* this *ought to be entertaining.*

"The fact that I don't fold and put away the laundry. I always assumed . . . I mean, I figured that once we were married . . . Anyway, I think it's their fault."

Kristen rolled her eyes. "I know you think it's the wife's job, Dave. Just say it. And yes, that may have been your family's system, but you're an adult now. Right?" She continued the movie—I swear I saw Hugh Grant wink at her—and I returned to my introspection. *That went well.*

I never intended to live like a male chauvinist. I don't consider myself to be one, yet prior to 2008 my de facto philosophies on the division of family labor would have suggested otherwise. My childhood seems to have had a lot to do with that.

My parents weren't chauvinists, but they were very traditional, in the traditional sense of the word. They each had clearly defined roles. They both worked—my dad was a farmer and my mom was an elementary school teacher—but it was understood that Mom was the domestic champion of the family. If women in Mayberry or Stepford did it, then my mom did it: cooking, cleaning, sewing, gardening. My brother and I only had to mow the lawn and help Dad around the farm—that was the extent of our contributions.

My dad didn't have to do much in the way of household chores. He would repair a toilet or wire a new outlet in the laundry room, but you'd never find him brandishing a toilet brush or sliding an iron across a pair of slacks. Although, in fairness, a few times a year I would spot my dad at the kitchen sink, doing dishes for my mom on the evenings when she could be found lying on their bed, tightly curled in on herself, suffering a migraine. I would stand silently in the doorway that separated the hallway from the kitchen, rubbing my fingertips along the glossy white molding, and watch him. He would first rinse a dish, then scrub it clean with soap and his bare hand, then repeat the process several times, making the dish spotless before setting it delicately and quite deliberately into its designated place in the dishwasher. Cleaning the kitchen after dinner for four people could take my dad all night; it would have taken my mom about ten minutes. Everything done in a certain way—like father, like son.

Then there was laundry. The laundry system with which I grew up was simple in terms of my participation therein. I'd observed that my mom almost never washed items left on my bedroom floor, but the tall wicker hamper that she placed in our bathroom was serviced regularly—at least twice per week, usually more. So when I needed something washed, it went into the hamper, and a few days later it would appear with its buddies on my bed, the whole lot of garments individually folded and stacked into neat piles. If she saw that the hamper wasn't quite full, she'd go out of her way to find me and ask if there was anything else I needed washed. Later that evening, my à la carte laundry order would be delivered to my bedroom, perfectly folded by my wiped-out mom.

"Here you go, sweetie," she'd say, handing me the clothes and kissing my forehead. "I'm exhausted. Good night." Then I'd set them on top of my dresser, knowing that by the same time the following day, as if by magic, the clothes would have made their way into their respective drawers.

That's what I call doing laundry, and for the longest time, I was puzzled that Kristen didn't operate the same way.

When we first moved in together, I tried making things easy on Kristen by instituting a hamper system similar to the one with which I'd grown up. However, my married-adult hamper system differed somewhat. For starters, I located the hamper in the bedroom closet rather than in our tiny master bathroom. The other difference was that Kristen didn't seem to give a shit about my clothes or my hamper.

I would load it up until it became a massive, unstable heap. I'd let a week go by without mentioning it, having learned that people who aren't my mom get sensitive about demands for personal service. My patience ran out whenever I'd find myself without clothes to wear to work, at which point I'd ask Kristen, "Were you planning to do the laundry at some point?" What can I say? The question always felt innocent enough, though looking back now it seems outrageously manipulative. I didn't mean to be passive-aggressive. I wasn't willfully imposing my antiquated worldview on her. I just thought that was how things worked. But how else was she supposed to have interpreted it? Had we known back then that I wasn't naturally equipped to adapt to someone else's system, this whole laundry situation might have been resolved sooner. As it was, I looked like an ass. I constantly found myself confused. *Am I an ass for assuming she'd do my laundry? Why wouldn't she do my laundry? The purview of a wife has always included laundry, has it not?*

To Kristen's credit, I'm still alive. Also to Kristen's credit, she would reply diplomatically to questions like mine, suggesting that if she was washing her own clothes, then I could throw my stuff in with hers. "Or, if you have clothes that need to be washed right now, you know how to do it," she'd always conclude. *Yes,* I'd think, standing there in my bottom-of-the-barrel emergency clothes (brown corduroy pants, a tight blue polo shirt, and black socks), *I know how to do it . . . but that's not the point!*

Due to what Kristen calls a "ridiculously high rate of sock-changings," I was constantly finding myself barefooted during our first year of marriage, so I eventually started washing my own clothes. That, too, became a problem. I was washing only my clothes, not hers. It didn't occur to me to wash everything together—why would it have? I don't wear her clothes, I wear my clothes. This easily could have been one of the questions on that Asperger's evaluation: *Do you need to be told explicitly to wash your wife's clothes if you're doing a load of laundry?* The follow-up questions being *Do you need to be told explicitly to fold the clothes when they're dry, even though you can explain the theory of relativity?* and *Wow, seriously?*

Perhaps a more telling question would be *Do you find it almost impossible to shed precepts and adapt to new ways of doing things?* Thanks to my Asperger's brain, the answer is an emphatic yes (especially when adapting means I'll be personally inconvenienced in some way), while an Asperger's-neutral question such as *Does it make sense that a person's gender dictates how they contribute around the house?* would garner a logical no. And yet, there I sat one evening, face-to-face with the lovable Hugh Grant and the realization that I had expected Kristen to do all the housework, just as my mom had.

Later that evening, well after the movie was finished, I would write in my journal, *Housework was my mom's job, but that doesn't mean it's Kristen's job.* I'd give serious thought to areas in which I could contribute. I would deem the toy room too chaotic for my involvement and therefore leave it to Kristen, but I would commit to continuing my responsibilities around the kitchen. I would design an hour-by-hour schedule for housework that would help me to stay on track, a list so unrealistic and unwieldy that we'd never be able to maintain it:

MONDAY

7:30 PM—Clean kitchen
8:30 PM—Vacuum and dust family room
9:30 PM—Iron blue dress shirts only

Ultimately, grimacing, I would commit in writing to folding and putting away the laundry.

But that would all come later. The movie was over now; the credits were rolling and I had some damage control to do. Kristen was sitting next to me, and next to her was a motley stack of linens topped with a bra. Because my previous attempts at talking had failed so miserably, I picked up my phone and texted her:

Hey [Send]

Her phone vibrated and she picked it up while I pretended not to look. A second later my phone buzzed:

hello.

I'm sorry I root through the dryer. You shouldn't have to fold everything [Send]

I'm used to it. :)

Put your hand out [Send]

Kristen slowly extended her hand in front of herself, as if she were reaching for something.

Give it to me over here, where I can reach it [Send]

The phone buzzed in her hand and this time she understood. Laughing, she lowered her hand, and I took it.

"I'm sorry," I said.

"For what?"

"For assuming that you would be responsible for all the housework."

"It's fine, Dave," she said. "Everyone has expectations. But you have to understand that there are other ways of doing things, and you need to learn how to open up to them."

"I will do more around the house. I just need to practice it, that's all."

"I'm not asking you to do much," she said. "I'm just saying that when you see clothes that need to be folded, you can fold them. When you see dishes that need to be washed or put away, you can do that. If there are toys on the floor, pick them up. That's all I'm saying."

You need me to be autonomous and learn how to adapt. You need me to be an adult. Ugh.

"Okay," I said. "I get it. I'm going to figure out a plan and then I'll get started working on it."

"I don't want you to spend a lot of time making plans and worrying about this," she said. "Don't make this a bigger deal than it needs to be. Just pick up, fold, put away. Help. That's it."

"Okay."

"Without pouting," she added.

"Pouting?" I picked up my phone.

:(Fuck you. [Send]

Chapter 6

Go with the flow.

Before we were married, Kristen and I lived with roommates for a year. They were friends of ours, and it seemed like such a good idea. It was one of those opportunities that neurotypicals might look forward to: a chance to celebrate and bond and party as only young, unmarried people with decent-paying jobs can—a yearlong last hurrah, and I missed it completely.

I wish I had enjoyed it more. Who knew living with friends could be such a disaster? They were, after all, good people, and as roommates go, they really weren't so bad.

I've had bad roommates. One of my college roommates, Derrick, wanted to kill me. That's not an exaggeration. He waited for me one morning in our room, and when I returned from my early classes, he shouted that he couldn't take any more of my shit and threatened to murder me if I didn't move out by the end of the week. "Can you give me another week at least?" I pleaded, holding up my calculus book with both hands to protect myself. "It's midterms."

"Fuck you, boy!" he boomed. "Fuck you, locking me out of the room at night!" *But I thought I made it clear that I lock the door at eleven thirty sharp, no matter what!* "Fuck you, waking me up every morning and telling me you're leaving!" *Isn't that just proper roommate etiquette?* "And fuck you for moving my shit around the bathroom! You don't touch another man's things, bitch! Fuck you!" *But your system was all wrong! Bar soap doesn't belong on a sink and toothbrushes should never be stored in a shower caddy!*

Derrick was strikingly muscular and I was mostly ribs and hair. Something about the volume of his voice and the way he was pacing the room, telling me that I didn't know who he was or where he came from, or what it was like to get "beat by an insane motherfucker"—it all seemed to suggest that he meant business. A couple of days later, after acing my calculus midterm (A+!), I moved in with a kid so inclined to talk about the time he'd spent working at the Target store in Eagan, Minnesota, that within a few weeks I'd started to reconsider my decision to move away from scary-ass Derrick.

A few months later I was bunking with Phill the percussionist, who despised and ridiculed the shape of my feet and listened to Jethro Tull at deafening volumes. After a two-week stretch in which he incessantly snapped the Morse code pattern for the word *marimba* with his fingers, I took a clerical job in the office of residence halls administration, which gave me a first look at all the prime single dorm rooms available on campus. At first, room turnover was slow, but I bided my time. Someone eventually requested a room change, and I helped myself to the fourteen-by-twelve single suite she was vacating. My new room was on a coed floor, across from a pair of dazzling Delta Gammas. Unpacking my milk crates, looking out over Lake Osceola and the music-school campus, and knowing that no roommate would be barging through the door while I typed up my letter of resignation to the residence halls administrator, I wondered how any student could ever walk away from such a beautiful room.

After Kristen and I started dating, I spent nearly every night at her house and never longed for the solitude of my own apartment. That was a first, and it proved that we cohabited well. She was the only person other than my family to earn that distinction. Growing up, I understood the power structure and everyone's role in the household: Mom and Dad were in charge and it was best not to challenge them. My brother was three years older, so he, too, could give me marching orders that I'd blindly accept if it meant he'd play with me ("Here, Dave, drink this paint thinner. Then we'll Hula-Hoop"). Most important, my family understood me. They loved me and accepted my little world for what it was. "Don't mind our son," my parents would say to guests as I pushed myself down the hallway floor on my face. The brushing sensation of blended-fiber carpet pile against my forehead put me in a place of tranquillity that to this day I can't achieve with sex, drugs, love, or money. Their guests would cautiously step back against the wall, allowing me to pass. "That's just our Dave."

I didn't have to worry about the sounds that escaped from my head. I had always mimicked the sounds of my environment, so even when I was older a few moos and quacks here and there didn't seem out of place. Using the corner of my mouth, I would serenade my mom with a perfectly rendered trombone solo as she sat barefoot at the kitchen table, watching *I Love Lucy* reruns and paying bills. Sometimes she would turn down the volume on the TV and snap her fingers in time, or set her checkbook down and just watch me; if I became self-aware, I'd run upstairs and press my forehead against the cool glass of my bedroom window. Because we lived on a farm, I could get lost in a daydream and wander off for hours without anyone thinking to bother me. If they did come looking, they weren't surprised when they found me standing motionless, expressionless, watching the wind pluck through the lilac bushes, or sitting alone in a cattle pen, tying individual strands of hay together. "Oh, there you are, Dave," my dad would say with a smile, his steely blue eyes sparkling the way they often did when he was amused. "Supper's almost ready, come and get washed up."

Some behaviors were too obnoxious for my family to tolerate.

High-pitched shrieking, lunging forward and backward, rewinding the same banal movie passage over and over. My mom would reach her threshold and firmly tell me to stop. In my dad, who was normally gentle and reserved, these types of behaviors provoked a different reaction. When he thought I was out of control, his face showed it—frustration, disapproval, anger. He hardly ever had to say anything. I drew my own conclusions about what he was thinking whenever he'd thunder away from me, growling, "Well, for Christ's sake." Namely, that I was a disappointment. The swish of his blue jeans accompanied him, whispering accusations at me above the stomping: *Well . . . now . . . you've . . . done . . . it . . .* After I frustrated him I wouldn't see him for hours. I would hide in my closet, or behind an open door, and mentally replay whatever had happened over and over, forcing promises upon myself to never be annoying again.

After a blissful first year of dating, and having decided that marriage was in our future, Kristen and I began playing with the idea of buying a house together. At first, we viewed the idea as a practical next step in our relationship. "I think it would make sense to find something now, even if it's strictly an investment," Kristen said. I agreed, and as we began searching for properties, our conversations about real estate grew more and more romantic. "Ooh, here's a nice two-story," she said, showing me a listing online. "Look at that family room. Isn't that *so* us? Can't you just see us in there, playing games in front of the fireplace?" *A good investment, and I get to live with my hot girlfriend—just the two of us. Nice!* But Kristen had a different idea.

"What if we looked for a bigger place, and we each picked a friend to live there with us?"

I thought about it for a moment. "Would they pay us rent?"

Kristen seemed confused by this question, as though I'd completely missed her point. "Well, yeah. I suppose they would pay rent.

But I was thinking more about how fun it would be, all of us living together. Can you imagine?"

I considered the advantages of dividing a mortgage four ways. Yes, I could imagine having roommates.

I immediately thought of Delemont, an incredibly mathematical guy with whom I'd been friends since middle school. He ended up designing bridges—a job that's just barely challenging enough to keep his interest. We worked about ten minutes from each other and met at least twice a week to have lunch, talk about math, and recite lines from Chris Farley movies. He had dark, wild hair, the sort I imagined could easily clog a drain. That was a check in the minus column, to be sure, and there were other demerits to consider.

When we were younger, Delemont tended to be loud and belligerent, especially whenever he drank or got himself into a crowd of people. In school, he would do or say anything if you paid him—he ate wood chips and friends' goldfish for a quarter, and struck a science teacher over the head with a textbook for a dollar. He didn't do these things because he needed the money; he did them because he needed to be outrageous—a motivation that I understood and admired. By the time he finished grad school, he had mellowed out somewhat, but his lack of regard for authority and rules in which he personally did not believe remained. Those weren't the types of qualities I'd normally look for in a roommate.

Still, Delemont had a capacity for friendship and decency that could make this plan work. In high school, during open gym, some skid mark of a kid was teasing me about how little I could bench-press. He wouldn't let up. I had tuned him out to study the tiny rhombuses etched into the grip of the weight bar when Delemont went crazy on the kid—getting in his face, yelling at him until a crowd gathered, then demanding that Skid Mark get on the bench and show everyone his highest weight. "*You* do it! Come on, big shot! Let's see *you* do it!" He stayed on Skid Mark like a pit bull and since then I've remained loyal to Delemont, who also appreciates a fine rhombus when he sees one.

Kristen agreed that Delemont would make a good choice and then revealed her selection. "I'm going to ask Meredith," she said.

Kristen had been close friends with Meredith since college, when they became sorority sisters. Meredith also had dark, wildish hair, though it was prettier than Delemont's, and she had a big, booming laugh that I figured I'd be hearing a lot of. At least, I hoped I'd hear a lot of it. I'd gotten along great with Meredith the few times we'd hung out, when I only had to be some exceptional version of myself to get through the evening. But living with her would present an entirely new set of demands. Full-time demands. For starters, she spoke as fast as lightning. Were she to tell me something important as I snapped a green bean, I'd miss it completely. I also worried that she would get to know me and realize that she didn't like me. Kristen dismissed the idea, but I had more concerns, none of which I voiced. *Will I be expected to hang out with both of them all the time? What if Meredith needs time with Kristen when I need time with Kristen? What if they start an inside joke and they don't let me in on it? What if Meredith takes huge dumps? Will I be forced to plunge her way out of it? Good God, I don't want to know that about a sorority girl.*

A week later, we asked Delemont and Meredith if they'd be interested in living with us. Kristen's conversation with Meredith went precisely like this:

Kristen: "Dave and I are buying a house and you're totally moving in with us!"

Meredith: "Oh my God! Fun!"

That was it. That was their entire discussion.

Delemont and I took a different approach, belaboring the strategy and logistics as only engineers and lunatics would. Discussing geography over lunch one day, we used a french fry to trace a series of ketchup arcs that represented ideal, acceptable, and unacceptable distances from our respective hamburger and hot dog offices, which we then analyzed against real estate prices.

It took some time to convince him, as there were plenty of cheap apartments within walking distance of his office. What ultimately sold him was the idea of living one last time with a group of friends.

"I think it will be fun living together," he said. "After living with my parents, some freedom will be nice. Just try to find something in this second ketchup arc."

A month later, Kristen and I found a three-story town house with two bedrooms and two full bathrooms upstairs, a beautiful kitchen, family room, and dining room on the main floor, and a full basement finished as an apartment. The location suited our commutes, so we arranged a visit with a real estate agent. Kristen fell in love immediately. She floated from room to room, lifted in reverie, suggesting who might sleep where and how we might arrange our new furniture, while I hunted for substandard craftsmanship and structural problems. We spent all of ten minutes in the house before Kristen announced, "This is the one. This is our home."

And so it was. We were thrilled. Everything about the house was perfect—even the walls were pristine. The rooms had been tastefully painted, and the upper floors had these great picture windows that looked out onto the large pond in the backyard, and into the woods beyond that.

Kristen and I moved in a week before anyone else and felt at home right away. In the mornings, we'd open the windows in the breakfast nook and listen to the faint whispers of blowing leaves and wind chimes. Late in the afternoon, sunlight would pour in through the windows in the family room and spread across the rich oak floors, causing them to glow, illuminating the bottom of our dark leather furniture. Fifteen minutes would pass in an instant as I'd stand in one place, mesmerized, staring at the floor. Kristen had been right—this was our home.

Then our friends moved in.

I wanted to be easy to live with. Really, I did. If I ever end up on trial for being a pain in the ass, prosecution's Exhibit A will be the

111

two-page memorandum I circulated to our roommates before they arrived. It was Asperger syndrome in its purest form, delivered in four excruciatingly long and schizophrenic bullet points and an anxious half-page conclusion. The first two points essentially read *Let's have fun this year* and *Let's remember that we're friends—it's best to keep the lines of communication open.* The latter half of the memorandum read like this: *On second thought, let's not overdo it on the communication—it's probably best to give each other plenty of space* and *Actually, let's not overdo it on the fun, either. And don't damage anything.* I had intended to convey to my new roommates just how easy and comfortable our living arrangement *could* be, as long as we all adhered to a few simple guidelines—*my* guidelines.

Delemont and Meredith were remarkably generous, saying only, "Does Kristen know you sent us this?" and "I think most of the guidelines in your memo go without saying." The latter was probably a reference to my prohibition of major renovations and rowdy all-night parties. Everyone seemed to be on the same page. Almost.

I'd asked our new roomies to refrain from hanging picture frames on "my pristine new walls," which left a giant loophole for Delemont, who skirted my request by nailing a dozen frameless pictures of bridges around his room shortly after he moved in. "You said no picture *frames,*" he said, proudly extending a gigantic middle finger to me and my policies, and my rage ignited. Rather than confronting him directly, I spent several days bemoaning Delemont's actions to anyone who would listen and being short and dismissive with everyone else. I was standing outside on the deck with Kristen when she decided she'd had enough of my moping.

"Dave, I understand that you're upset with Delemont and his nails, but can you please tell me why it's a big deal to you?" she asked.

"What can I say, Kristen? He's completely fucking insane. Who nails pictures to walls? Pictures that he tore from a fucking *calendar* about *bridges!*"

"Delemont does, I guess. But I still don't get what you're so angry about." Meredith spotted Kristen and me from the kitchen and wandered out to join us.

"Kristen, nails leave holes. The house that you and I bought last month didn't have nail holes; it was spotless. Now, in partial custody of a crazy person, it does. I didn't put them there, you didn't put them there. *He* put them there." *Great, now I look crazy. Can't you just agree that this is a huge deal and that my anger is 100 percent his fault? He is to blame. He is to be questioned, not me! I'm the victim!*

"Right." I knew she couldn't see my point, and I wasn't sure how to proceed with Meredith standing right next to me. Around her, I had always played the role of Kristen's Charming Boyfriend—my favorite character—but that guy was nowhere to be found.

"Are you guys talking about Delemont's bridge pictures? What's up with those?" Meredith asked.

I couldn't keep myself from ranting. "Look, what if we had a baby and he came over and pierced her ears? Wouldn't you be pissed off?"

"I'm not sure if I'd call that the same thing," Kristen said.

How is that not the same thing?!

"I think you'll be able to paint over the holes easily enough," Meredith offered.

That's when I snapped.

"Oh, that's fucking great, Meredith! We'll just paint over it. No problem, right? Grab a fucking hammer and let's smash some walls! No big deal, right?" I snatched Delemont's cigarette lighter from the patio table and chucked it into the grass below. "Fuck all this!" I reared back to kick the table, but then I saw Kristen's face. I'd never seen her look more stunned or horrified. I didn't even bother looking at Meredith. Suddenly, my head was spinning and I couldn't take myself or them. I barged past Meredith, stormed inside, and went upstairs to our room.

Fuck.

I'd gotten that stunned *What just happened?!* look millions of times before—from teachers, from my parents, from friends—but never from Kristen. She had just caught her first glimpse of her fiancé going from zero to boiling in an instant, with no legitimate provocation. For more than a year—scratch that, for more than a decade—I had managed to conceal from Kristen my hardwired incapacity to deal with things like nail holes and anger. I had always kept myself in check around her, and then suddenly this happened.

To Kristen, nail holes were no more significant than fingerprints on the doorknobs or dust on the carpet. To her, such intense anger about something so superficial was far more damaging than the holes themselves. But I didn't get that. All I saw was her face during my outburst, her expression and speechlessness mirroring my desperation. For the first time, I didn't feel like the life of her party, and I hated myself for it. *Great. Nice job, shithead. Mer just got it, too—that's perfect. Game over. You're the freak now, and they're all going to hate you. Happy? Happy, fucker?* I just wanted to crawl into my old closet at my parents' farmhouse, or push myself facedown through the halls to my old hiding spot behind the dining room door, and wait for the episode to leave my head. *Fucking Delemont.*

Kristen eventually joined me on our bed to talk about what had happened. Had we known that I had Asperger's, there wouldn't have been so much confusion. We might have known that I tend to feel a greater emotional connection to inanimate objects, like walls, than I do to most people. We might have known that a sense of order and control was critically important to me. We might have known that my brain wasn't built to tolerate reality when reality doesn't match my expectations. Circumstances being what they were, however, an explanation was in order.

"Everything okay?" she asked.

I was too ashamed to look at her, so I stared at the wall and nodded.

"Is this really about a few nail holes? Or is there something else?"

"Today it's about nail holes. But what about tomorrow? It might be wild parties, complete strangers driving motorcycles through our house. There's no control. I can't deal with this."

Kristen laughed. "So, today's nails open the door for tomorrow's home-obliterating motorcycle parties?"

I couldn't laugh with her because it made perfect sense to me. *Of course! Duh.* She tried explaining the difference between reacting and overreacting, saying, "It's natural to get upset about things. I was just surprised by the intensity of your anger. You can get mad, but it's not okay to get so mad that you lose control." I understood her point, but I couldn't imagine myself reacting any differently.

"I don't know what my problem is," I said. "I just can't handle this."

"Dave, I think you just need to relax. This whole year is about having fun. We just have to let some things slide. Okay?"

I said okay, as I would hundreds of times that year when being told exactly the same thing. You have to relax. You have to pick your battles. Let's just enjoy this. "Okay." *But how?*

The year progressed without any more nail holes, without the dreaded wild parties, and without any crazed motorcyclists cutting donuts on our immaculate oak floors. (It's worth mentioning, however, that Kristen cut a deep four-foot scratch into the kitchen floor by accident, and unlike Delemont's nail holes, there was no way to repair it without full replacement. Yet I managed to laugh that one off. Forgiveness is easy when you're in love.)

But that's not to say that things got any easier. Meredith contracted conjunctivitis—pinkeye—and I quarantined her for days. It wasn't a formal quarantine; she had simply gotten the hint that I was fearful of contamination when she saw my hand, protected by a latex glove, slipping a list of nearby hotels with phone numbers under her door after I found out that her eye was crusted shut with pus. "The antibiotics I've been given make it impossible to spread," she insisted from behind her closed door. But come on. That's just ridiculous.

Worse than exposing my aversion to bacterial infections, however, was the fact that I never quite figured out how to cope with the social dynamics of the household. My failures in dealing with group situations began taking a toll on both Kristen and me. Spending time with Delemont or Meredith individually was never a problem. I knew that the key to hanging out with Delemont was always to talk sincerely and literally, to include tremendous detail, and to tell highly exaggerated jokes. I eventually learned how to manage Meredith as well. Details seemed to confuse her, as did having to repeat herself ("Wait, repeat which part? What was I saying again?"), so I learned to get to the point quickly and then activate hyper-listening in preparation for her astoundingly fast-spoken response.

But these techniques for one-on-one engagement flew out the window whenever we convened as a group. Game nights, especially, were ripe for disaster. For weeks, we followed a particular sequence of games: Catch Phrase! followed by Scattergories, followed by Kristen and Meredith gossiping to each other while Delemont and I played Mastermind. I'm not sure if anyone else noticed this pattern, but I sure did; the routine had become as essential to game night as the games themselves. When someone suggested a new game, or when the group decided to change the sequence, I couldn't handle it. *Scrabble?!* I would participate in the games, but my lifelong pattern of scowling and brooding in response to a change in routine would take hold of my behavior. I would grow silent and passively belligerent: *We always start with Catch Phrase!, and they know that, so why are we mixing it up?* Delemont might laugh about something, then look to me to keep the joke going, and I'd snub him by asking if we were still playing. "Well, are we? Because I thought this was game night. So, whose turn?" If someone asked me what was wrong, I'd say that nothing was wrong and then grow even quieter.

The fun would plow forward without me, and my anger would turn inward: *You're only ruining this for yourself, dumbass. They think you're a jerk, and they're right.* Kristen and our roommates would assume that I was angry with them, although I thought that I could trick them into thinking I was crabby about something else. They knew me better than that. "Dave, what's the problem? Why are you pissed at everybody?" Kristen would whisper. *I don't even know.*

We'd end the evening early, Delemont and Meredith would return to their rooms, and Kristen would be disappointed with me—her sulking fiancé, who should have been enjoying the company of friends. "Is it impossible for you to have fun now?" she'd ask, and I'd tell her to forget it. The awkward evening, with all my mistakes, would play in a constant loop in my head for days until something would happen, for instance dropping my phone, and then I'd melt down. Sometimes I would sit in my car, furious at myself for making everything so hard, sobbing uncontrollably, slapping myself in the face over and over and screaming, "Fucking asshole! Fucking asshole!" But who hasn't done *that* from time to time?

The fact that I used to sit around in my car and punch myself in the face after a rough night of Scattergories should have been a clear indication that something was amiss. It wasn't until years later, however, that I'd understand the underlying problem: I didn't know how to go with the flow. As life skills go, adaptability is perhaps one of the most essential. Things happen unexpectedly or they don't always break in your favor, and maintaining composure under those circumstances is often the only way to get through them with your sanity intact. Unfortunately, those of us with Asperger syndrome tend to be short on flexibility, just as we are on empathy and conversational give-and-take. (If you're keeping score at home, that's Asperger's three, marriage zero.)

This natural disinclination to go with the flow made living with me almost unbearable for Kristen and our roommates. Back then I was jeopardizing friendships with my emotional outbursts, but as time went on, the stakes became much higher. My inability to cope with real life and the resultant anger it fostered made me, if not an unreliable marital partner, then certainly an unpleasant one. And it didn't take long for my status as a husband to erode from "unpleasant" to "unworthy," all because of my inability to deal. Going with the flow was especially important after we had kids and life became truly unpredictable. As infants, Emily and Parker didn't seem too concerned about my daily routine. My days amounted to a series of interruptions. As the kids grew, they took cues from our behaviors as to how they should react to things, and as someone who lost his mind over hamburger buns, I was not a very suitable role model. With our children's development at stake, it was more important than ever to learn how to minimize the damaging outbursts and behaviors.

Fortunately, the kids and I had Kristen to show us how to roll with life's punches and how to do it with a smile. "What can you do?" she'd say with a shrug, heating up a steamy shower at three A.M. if one of the kids was suffering a croupy cough. Almost as a matter of protocol, I'd insist that we head straight to the emergency room (just as I did whenever one of them bumped their knee or had a runny nose), and with wet hair clinging to the sides of her face and a toddler nearly asleep on her hip, she'd stop her gentle lullaby to comfort me, saying, "If it gets worse, we'll go. But I think the cough sounds better, don't you?"

Kristen had expected our year living with Delemont and Meredith to be one of the happiest years of our life together—a dream that exploded in her face because of my failure to adapt. While someone else might have packed her things and left, Kristen didn't give up on me. Instead, she handled it with her usual grace. Not gracefulness, not finesse, but authentic grace that she bestowed on me even though I hadn't earned it.

After our roommates moved out, it occurred to me that I had run out of opportunities to enjoy living with them. I apologized to Kristen for ruining the entire year and she shrugged it off. "This year was a disappointment, but then again, I didn't know how challenging it would be for you." Then her eyes brightened, and she added, "We're getting married in a month, and then we'll have lots of opportunities to enjoy things together. So let's just relax and have fun."

That's how Kristen handles things. She doesn't look backward, only forward. In doing so, she had committed the ultimate act of going with the flow. It was a perfect model for me to follow, but of course, I failed to make that connection. And for years, I kept failing. She constantly had to remind me to chill out. The other cars got a green arrow and I didn't: "Relax, Dave. It happened four hours ago. You can't let it ruin the whole day." Emily ate a candle: "This isn't the end of the world, Dave. No, you don't need to fly home from Italy, she's fine." Both of our children proved to be terrified of people in costumes *after* we waited in line to buy tickets at Six Flags Great America: "Dave, oh well. Let's find something else they'll enjoy." "Okay," I would say. *But how?*

Sometimes I argued with her. "Going with the flow is for hobos and douchebags. It's for people without goals or vision. People with nothing to accomplish. Me, I'd rather accomplish things." She would insist that going with the flow wasn't about complacency or letting the tide carry you along. "People like you especially need to learn how to adapt," she'd tell me. "You do have your own vision, you do have goals to pursue. But life throws punches and if you don't roll with them, you'll get knocked down and you won't accomplish anything." For the longest time, her point failed to sink in, even when she put it bluntly: "I don't like being around you when you're flipping out over stupid stuff. Knock it off."

Her message finally clicked for me in the fall of 2008. I was sitting on the floor in our family room, trying to make good on my most recent Best Practice: folding laundry. I had a meeting with my sales director the following morning, and I was watching *SportsCenter* on ESPN in preparation for his inevitable sports banter—sort of like cramming for an exam. The show's anchor made a reference to one of the greatest tennis champions of all time, Roger Federer, and as I squared up a pair of boxers, I took a moment to wonder what it must be like to be the best at something: *This Federer can't lose—he just wins all the time. Well, not all the time. I guess he can't win every point. He doesn't win every game, actually, or even every match. But he's the best—I like that. Federer knows what he needs to do and he doesn't let a bad call or a loss bring him down and . . . OHHHH!*

I scrambled up the steps and into our bedroom, waking Kristen to share my epiphany:

"I was watching sports highlights and it all makes perfect sense now! Go with the flow! Pick the battles! Let things slide! I don't, so every day we're putting out some big drama fire. I wish I would have realized this years ago!"

"Sports highlights taught you this?" she asked. "Really, Dave?"

"I know you've told me this six million times, but it's so clear to me now! I think I'm onto something!"

"That's great," she mumbled. "I'm happy for you."

That was the most enthusiasm I was going to rally from Kristen given the time of night, so I grabbed my notebook from my nightstand drawer and—in a manner of speaking—teed off. A highlight reel of my journal entry that evening might look something like this:

> *Go with the flow.*
>
> *Purpose—Flexibility is an essential social skill, like communication. Being inflexible prevents me from experiencing joy which is right in front me. It stresses me out. My failure to adapt has driven a wedge between Kristen and me. It's making me a bad role model for my kids.*
>
> *Payoff—If I can learn to go with the flow, then I will be a more*

stable husband and father. I won't have to live in a constant state of agitation. I may start enjoying things!

Process—Start by learning to pick the battles. Learn the difference between critical and favorable outcomes. Emily and Parker never, ever coloring on the walls with crayon would be favorable. Raising kids who don't flip out every time something goes wrong—leading by example—is critical. If necessary, ask Kristen to help define what's important.

The storm of ideas and dot-connecting finally let up around two A.M., and rather than finishing the laundry, I went back to the beginning of my entry and thought about what I'd written. Going with the flow was shaping up to be an essential behavioral goal, on a par with *Be her friend, first and always.* Which worried me, because going with the flow was clearly against my nature. Then again, if I were relying solely on Best Instincts, there would be nothing to practice.

I can do this, I thought. *There are so many areas in my life that will improve by going with the flow. There's no telling how much of a game changer this is going to be.*

Chapter 7

When necessary, redefine perfection.

O ne night not long after my *SportsCenter* epiphany, life handed me a test. Looking back, it was more of a pop quiz with one question: *So, you think you can go with the flow?* Kristen and I were visiting our friends Andy and his wife, Mary, who live next door to us. Andy and I are polar opposites. He is muscular, laid-back, and has a nose stolen from a Roman statue, while I am skinny, neurotic, and have a nose that sometimes whistles when I make out. But we've been close friends since kindergarten, when we both witnessed a girl eat a handful of pumpkin seeds during a pumpkin-carving project and immediately throw them back up. We were the only kids who cheered; everybody else freaked out. In high school, I wrote poems about mathematics and dreamed up marching band configurations while Andy played team sports and made new friends. That's when he met Mary, and they've been together ever since, more than half of their lives.

Kristen and Mary were both pregnant when we all decided to build houses right next to each other, in a new subdivision situated on what used to be a vast piece of cropland. (I had driven plows through a patch of soil not far from where our houses now stand, so I have to laugh when my neighbors refer to their riding lawn mowers as "tractors.") The developer planted some scrawny saplings along each street, which ought to look pretty nice in about fifty years. But for now, the absence of real trees only draws attention to the homogeneity of our neighborhood. Everything looks the same from the outside—two-story houses with tan vinyl siding or brick facades and cedar fences. It's all very cookie-cutter. Andy and Mary went with siding, Kristen and I chose brick, and our floor plans differ somewhat. But in terms of looks, that's where dissimilarity ends. Our floors, countertops, kitchen cabinets, and bathrooms all look identical, which makes it easy for me to feel comfortable when I'm in their house.

Unlike certain other of my living arrangements, moving next door to Andy and Mary proved to be a great idea. We were guaranteed a good neighbor, for one thing, but living side by side also made it fantastically easy to visit them.

It was Andy's birthday and Mary had planned a quiet little get-together for him that evening. Just his parents, his family, and our family celebrating the occasion over ice cream and an impressive homemade layer cake with chocolate frosting in the middle.

Mary was handing me my plate when Kristen took a bite and cried out, "Oh my God, this cake is *amazing*!" Andy nodded, his frosting-smeared mouth too full to say anything, while his parents agreed: "It's really good, Mary."

"You made this, Mary?" Kristen asked. "Dave, try some."

I took a bite and rolled my eyes. "*This* is what all other cakes should strive to be."

Mary had spent a good portion of the day making the cake and Andy's favorite dinner, pork tenderloin, but according to Andy she didn't let that interfere with her normal routine of cleaning the house, playing with their kids, and working out.

Kristen chuckled from across the room. "Poor Dave. He never

gets pork tenderloin and cake on his birthday. Not unless we go to his parents' house. Sorry, hon." Everyone laughed but me. I chewed my lip, trying not to compare Andy's typical day with mine—the housework he wasn't obligated to help with, the amazing meals he got to eat, the buttons sewn back onto his shirts for free. Kristen winked at me, and rather than playing along, I helped myself to another serving of Mary's cake. I might have found Kristen's little joke amusing had we not eaten cold cereal for lunch that day.

Kristen and I returned home to our day's messes—the dishes piled high in the sink, the random books and magazines sitting on the couch next to a flashlight and an empty box, the kids' toys scattered across every room. *Good lord.* Kristen took the kids upstairs for bed while I straightened up a bit. Mary had sent us home with cake, and I was searching our dirty, crowded refrigerator for someplace to put it when Kristen came downstairs and asked me why I was being so crabby.

I didn't want to get involved in an argument, so I lied, saying that I wasn't being crabby at all, I was just looking for a goddamn place to set the cake down in our disgusting pit of a refrigerator. "That's all."

"Come on, Dave," she said. "Use your words."

Fine. I removed some cartons of leftover Thai food to make room for our miracle cake and shut the door. *Let's have some words.*

"You know what, Kristen? A few weeks ago, I thought that I had come to terms with my expectations for you as a homemaker. I thought I had all that shit figured out—it's not your job to do that stuff, it's everyone's responsibility to pitch in. So I've been helping with the laundry and I've been feeling okay. Then, tonight, we go next door and I see every one of my expectations for you being realized at every turn with someone else. Mary's cooking up pork and baking a cake and vacuuming and God knows what else they're up to over there. I thought I had this shit under control two weeks ago, but apparently, I don't. I don't. I'm admitting it right now, and it's ugly, and it's not fair to you, and it makes me feel like a real asshole, but there it is."

She could have stormed out. She could have agreed and called me an asshole. Instead, she nodded the way she does when I'm telling her something she already knows.

"So, you want me to be just like Mary?"

Do I? I paused, wondering. Part of me wanted to say yes, but another part of me wanted to be happy with what we had. Kristen and I weren't complete failures when it came to running a household. It wasn't as if our house was filthy, it just wasn't always "company-ready," as my mom would say. Our house was always clean *enough*—no more, no less. Same with meals. Kristen made sure the kids ate healthy foods for meals and snacks, and when she wasn't at work she kept them on a loose but reliable schedule: breakfast, lunch, and dinner served at the usual times, with snacks in between. But we never ate together as a family. Most nights, I had no idea when I'd be home from work. Plus, Kristen and I found that we could enjoy our dinners in peace if we waited until after the kids were asleep. One of us would usually start cooking something simple—pasta, tacos, that sort of thing—at around eight thirty. But that was purely for my sake. Kristen made it clear that she would have been perfectly content to eat olives right out of the can for dinner, but I insisted on hot food, served on a plate. "Like real people," I told her.

Because she wasn't in the habit of planning meals, Kristen rarely took care of the grocery shopping. We'd start making tacos and realize halfway into the process that we had no cheese or taco shells, and so I'd find myself driving to the grocery store at nine or later—when it seems very few decent people are out shopping. I'd return from the store, we'd finally eat dinner, and then she would turn on her computer and work until she couldn't stay awake any longer. Reports had to be written, invoices had to be submitted, questions from her husband like "Aren't you going to do the dishes?" had to be graciously ignored. She allocated little bandwidth to domestic greatness because bandwidth was scarce and necessarily limited to domestic functionalism. It was perfectly understandable, but I had been raised to expect that a home would be managed better than that.

"You know that being a homemaker isn't my highest priority," Kristen told me, reaching into the refrigerator and plucking a smidgen of frosting from the miracle cake. "For some women, like Mary, it is. And God bless them for it, because it is a lot of work. But I've got you to put up with—that takes most of my energy right there."

"I don't want you to suddenly turn into Mary," I said. "But I expected that you would naturally be like her, and it's still messing me up."

"I get that, but let's face it: You're saying Mary's perfect, right?"

I hesitated to comment, although there was plenty of evidence to support Kristen's statement. For as long as I've known Mary, she has seemed perfect. In high school she graduated third in our class, was a fantastic swimmer, remembered birthdays, and was nice to everybody. In college, she was a perfect straight-A student, still remembered birthdays, and was still nice to everybody. After college, she couldn't wait to start her life with Andy—she was excited to be his perfect wife. Now, as an adult with children of her own, Mary is the perfect stay-at-home mom. She keeps their house immaculate and every time I'm there it smells like whatever new, fabulous meal she's been preparing from scratch.

Mary does more than take care of her own family. In addition to her own kids, she also takes care of ours and a few others from around the neighborhood. Yet she never looks tired or frazzled. When we pick up our kids in the afternoon, Mary hands us an activity sheet that chronicles their day: what the kids ate for morning snack, what they ate for lunch, what they ate for afternoon snack, how long they napped, when they had diaper changes and trips to the potty. Everything's on the sheet, including what they did for fun: *We read books and played dress-up all morning. At noon, the weather was nice so we went on a picnic at the park. Afterward, we sang songs, made alphabet letters out of bread dough, and rode bikes.*

Things always run according to plan in Andy and Mary's house. Meals, for instance, are served promptly at seven thirty, noon, and six o'clock, and they all eat together. On Mary's pristine kitchen counter-top, next to the tidy stacks of incoming and outgoing mail, lies her meticulous family schedule.

Tuesday 1:00 P.M.—~~Clothes shopping for kids *Note: sale at Carter's, bring coupons~~
Tuesday 2:00 P.M.—~~Drive home *Note: be home by 2:50 to defrost meat~~
Tuesday 3:00 P.M.—Defrost meat / Clean toy room

If you were to exit through Andy and Mary's front door, turn right, and walk a hundred feet to our house, you'd find just the opposite. We're not the sort of people who have a schedule or even a to-do list, but if we were, you might find it scrawled across a takeout napkin, and it would include such things as *Fish cell phone out of garbage disposal. Figure out where the car seats went. Pay water bill, ask city to turn water back on.*

"I'm saying Mary's an ideal homemaker," I said. "But I'm not asking you to become a domestic goddess—that's not my point. My point is that I don't *want* to expect that from you anymore. I'm trying to change myself here, not you. Tonight was just a setback."

"Whatever," Kristen said, leaning in for a kiss. "It's fine. Good night."

She yawned and headed upstairs for bed, while I stayed in the kitchen and helped myself to yet another piece of Mary's cake.

The next morning, I awoke to Kristen kissing me on the forehead, telling me she had to go to work. "The kids are ready to go to Mary's. Can you take them?"

I nodded into my pillow, blinded by the sunlight streaming in through our bedroom windows.

"Thanks," she said. "I love you."

"Love you, too." *Okay—last night was a setback. That's all. Time to get back on track.*

I navigated through the usual morning chaos with the kids—more cereal please; not that kind of cereal; more water please; I meant juice; look, my pants are on my head; my shoes were in Mommy's purse so can I wear my rain boots—and at eight thirty, we headed next door.

"Is Kristen working early this morning?" Mary asked as she helped me to remove the kids' shoes and jackets.

"Yeah, and I did not sleep well last night."

"How come?"

I hugged the kids and they ran off into Mary's toy room, which was clean and organized and filled wall-to-wall with books and games and crafts. The house already smelled like pot roast, and Mary—who looks so much like Kristen that they're sometimes mistaken for sisters—looked as fresh and relaxed as ever.

"Who knows," I said.

Mary laughed and asked if it was because I'd eaten so much cake the night before, and then she abruptly marched into the kitchen, saying: "Wait here a second. I have something for you guys."

I stood in the foyer while she continued talking to me from the kitchen, and I noticed how few decorations they had in their entryway compared with the rest of their house. There were pictures and mementos scattered throughout the other rooms, and the one that stood out was a hand-painted rendition of a poem that Andy's sister had written for them as a wedding gift. The words escape me, but the gist was that their love shades the path of their life, like trees growing over a road. Something like that. It was heartfelt and affecting, and when Kristen and I weren't getting along, any thought of that poem aggravated me. There were some trees painted in the background and the entire work was framed and displayed above their formal living room love seat.

The closest thing we had to a handmade emblem of our love was a torn sticker on Kristen's rearview mirror. It read PRINCESS, KRISTEN. When we were dating I had printed this on a label maker at work. The original sticker read THE PERFECTLY IMPERFECT PRINCESS, KRISTEN. I'd created it in response to a label she had given to me after I'd gotten emotional talking about how happy I was to be with her. YOU ARE SUCH A GIRL, it read. My first response read YOU ARE SUCH A BITCH. I tossed that in the trash. Too risky. Then I made the princess label. When I gave it to her, she tore off the part she liked best and stuck it on her mirror. No frame. No trees. Just pure label-maker romance.

In Andy and Mary's family room there were frames and shadow-boxes almost everywhere the eye landed. Inside each one was a picture of them being a super couple: relaxing on the beach in Hawaii; smiling at each other on their wedding day; laughing with their heads comi-cally and gender-swappingly misplaced into the circular facial cutouts of a male bodybuilder and a platinum-blond calendar girl painted on a sheet of plywood.

Kristen and I didn't do shadowboxes, and for years there were no pictures displayed of us or even the kids. Our bare walls said a lot about who we were as a couple and as a family, just as Andy and Mary's prominently displayed family portraits spoke volumes about them. That's not to say that we didn't have any photos of good times. We had a couple of candid shots taken at arm's length in a Salt Lake City parking garage, stashed in a drawer. I sometimes found them when I was looking for a coaster. We also had wedding pictures, but I had never gotten around to picking them up from the photographer's studio.

Mary returned, handing me a Tupperware container. "I made some more of that salsa that Kristen likes," she said. "This batch isn't as tomato-y as the other one, just so she knows. But Andy tried some last night and he loved it." For a moment I felt envy rising, and I noticed a pattern emerging. *Things are fine at home, then I come here and get a soul-crushing glimpse of perfection. We may have to move.*

I thanked her, and she said with all the sincerity in the world, "It's no problem. Hope she likes it." I returned home with the salsa and texted Kristen:

> Mary made u salsa. I'll put it in the fridge.

She didn't respond, so I sent another one:

> Didn't give us chips to go with it tho—guess she's not perfect.

That got a response:

> She's probably making the chips by hand.

I spent the following week trying not to think too much about the disparity in Kristen's and Mary's priorities. But comparison is a compulsively playable game, and a dangerous one. The more I compared Kristen's résumé as a homemaker to Mary's, the more I started to compare my overall relationship with Kristen to that of Andy and Mary—an exercise that was sure to sow disappointment.

It's worth mentioning that I sometimes get stuck on strange and unfamiliar words—or rather, strange and unfamiliar words get stuck on me. In passing, I'll hear someone in my office say the word *fiduciary*, and before I have a chance to look it up in a dictionary, I'll have heard it six or seven more times throughout the day. In the elevator, on the radio, in line at the deli: *Fiduciary! There it is again!* I'm always left wondering, *Have people been saying this word all along? How have I not noticed this before?* Then, as swiftly as it came into my life, the word will vanish—sometimes for years. When it rains, it pours, I guess. It doesn't seem to matter if it's raining unfamiliar words or unpleasant reminders of personal circumstances.

The following Saturday, Kristen was trying to get caught up on work. When she told me she had been craving a peanut-butter-cup milk shake all day, I offered to run out and get one for her. She thanked me by setting her files aside and pulling me close for a long, cozy hug. Rubbing my hand in circles across her back, I smiled, thinking this was a small but certain indication that we were back on track. *Look at me fulfilling her needs. Look at us being sweet and romantic together.*

But then I made the mistake of calling Andy to see if he wanted to come with me.

"I can't right now, buddy," he said cheerfully. "Mary and I are reading the new Harry Potter to each other."

"Pardon me?"

He clarified that the book wasn't brand-new, it was just new to them. They hadn't read that one yet. But that was hardly the point.

"You *read* to each other?"

"Sure. That way, neither of us gets left out when we get a new book. And we just like to do this once in a while."

Oh, fuck me.

I got off the phone as quickly as possible, and Kristen asked me what was wrong. Apparently, the fact that I had rolled my eyes when I hung up had given me away. At first, I offered Kristen ten million guesses as to what was going on next door, but when she wouldn't play along, I simply gave her the answer:

"Harry fucking Potter, Kristen. They are sitting on their fucking couch, under a fucking blanket, reading Harry fucking Potter to each other."

Kristen did her best to stifle a laugh and asked why this posed such a problem for me. The problem, of course, was *who were they to be in such a happy marriage that they would actually sit and read books to each other?*

"Yeah, that's pretty unconscionable," she said. "How dare they?"

My logic was clearly lost on her, so I resorted to acting even more childishly. "Whatever, Kristen. Hey, tonight let's turn the clock back to the eighteen hundreds like Andy and Mary do, so we can read books to each other like shithead pioneers. Maybe if we did that then we'd actually look like a couple in love, like they do, and then we could stuff it down everyone's throats."

"Dave, knock it off. They're just doing what works *for them*. They're not stuffing anything down anyone's throats. My God, you're so jealous." She shook her head.

I didn't want to admit that Kristen was right. I knew that acknowledging my jealousy would mean acknowledging that I had a number of unfulfilled expectations. I didn't want to have to deal with more unfulfilled expectations; I just wanted to buy a milk shake. But I was jealous. Insanely jealous. By some fluke, Andy and Mary had been enjoying the marriage I had always wanted and expected. Mary taking care of the household. Andy reading to her under a blanket. The two of them finding time between balancing their checkbooks, maintaining their landscaping, and ironing their curtains to fall more and more in love with each other every day. Their marriage appeared to be blissful, stable, romantic. Not chaotic, not painful or confusing like ours had been, but perfect. To me, theirs was what a successful marriage looked like, and I couldn't help but notice that it looked a lot like the marriage my parents had.

My mom and dad didn't argue with each other. They were comfortable in their roles, just as Andy and Mary were. They ate and slept and shopped at regular hours, just like Andy and Mary. And they were constantly showering each other with affection, just like Andy and Mary. Every evening growing up, my brother and I would come downstairs on a homework break or in search of ice cream, and we'd find my parents giggling and hugging and carrying on like honeymooners. We'd observe this, watching their private moment, and then we'd squeeze in between them, absorbing all of their love like little freckled sponges.

My marriage was supposed to look like that. It wasn't supposed to involve cereal for lunch and other letdowns. It was supposed to be constant affection, not once-in-a-while, thanks-for-buying-me-a-shake affection. Andy and Mary had no business being so functional. They had no business being so matchy-matchy. They had no business being so happy.

"That's the problem," I told Kristen. "We don't read to each other. We don't hug or hold hands or swat each other with dish towels. We don't hang family pictures, because we don't have any. We spent five years arguing and totally disconnected. Five years! Andy and Mary are living in a perfect marriage, and we aren't."

"Dave, our marriage is perfect," she said. "If you could stop looking at what it was supposed to be and start looking at what it actually is, then you might see that." She waited a moment for my brain to catch up to her words, and then she smiled the way she smiles when she's done talking about something and wants to move on. "Now, go get my shake."

Two weeks later, I was standing on our front porch with a ladder and two boxes of Christmas decorations. The late autumn wind was more or less steady, with some gusts every now and then to remind me that it was below freezing outside. "Can you hurry? How long is this going to take you?" Kristen asked from the warmth of our foyer. I had about ninety minutes until nightfall.

"Not long."

Rather than opening my eyes to our version of perfect, as Kristen suggested, for the past two weeks I had been trying a different tack: seeking opportunities to lead us directly into what I considered to be a utopian marriage. *We are going to be happy and functional, damn it. I'll see to that personally.*

Something about hanging Christmas decorations had always

given me a sense that I was the head of a functional family. I think that's because a nicely decorated house is no accident. The decorations must be purchased in advance and stored year-round. Ladders are involved, as are special plastic clips and extension cords. All of which denote a certain degree of having one's shit together. It's easy to find satisfaction in the job, too. The sun goes down, the lights come on, and suddenly it's the holidays. Add a quiet snowfall, and you've got something resembling a Norman Rockwell portrait.

I schlepped my ladder over behind the bushes in front of our living room window and propped it up against the brick facade of our house. From the boxes on the porch, I removed two long strands of garland and Christmas lights, stretched them out across the yard, and plugged them in to check if the bulbs worked. Which they didn't. *Oh, for Christ's sake.* I looked next door. Andy and Mary were standing in their driveway, keeping warm in matching knitted caps, which I assumed Mary had picked out for the two of them. Their porch and garage were lit up with hundreds of tiny lights, and the fat spruce in the corner of their yard had been decorated to look like a Christmas tree. Mary was cheerfully helping Andy put up their decorations and laughing at something he had said.

"Hi, Dave," she called.

"Hey, buddies. I guess I have to go to the store to get more lights. Do you need anything?"

"You know you're almost out of daylight, right?" Andy asked, positioning his wooden reindeer between some bushes.

"Yeah, but I can finish this in time." *Fuckface.* "You know, I think Kristen and I will probably get started on the inside decorations this week."

"Just think," Andy said as his reindeer's nose lit up. "We've already put up our Christmas tree, decorated inside, and we're almost done with all the outside lights! But we'll let you know if we need anything from the store."

Mary laughed, hard, the way she might have laughed had I just tripped and fallen face-first into the crotch of their snowman. Then she gave Andy a playful hug, cuing him to back off a little bit. "You'll be fine, Dave, just ignore him." It was a nice thing for her to say, and it made me furious.

Fuck this. Maybe they are better than us. Comically better. Painfully, obviously, woefully better than us.

Then I turned my thoughts to Kristen. *Why isn't she outside helping me? Why can't she buy* us *matching hats?* My internal grousing was interrupted by one of our kids screaming inside, then a loud thud, and then more screaming. Through the front window I watched Kristen gather Parker up from the floor as she sent Emily, crying, to sit in time-out. I looked back at Andy's house. As I stared into the bright red nose of that cocksucking, smug little reindeer, it was easy to imagine their children inside, calmly reading books or practicing long division in a fragrant cloud of homemade gingerbread. Or perhaps from behind a frosted windowpane they'd sip eggnog and delight in watching the doofus next door tripping over himself.

Kristen opened the door and the screams of our children's tantrums echoed off nearby houses. "How's it going out here, Dave?" she asked. She didn't mean for me to give her an update on my progress, she meant, *It's a zoo in here, I need your help, pick up the pace.*

I shrugged.

"It's going shitty, isn't it?" She rolled her eyes and slammed the door. *Perfect.*

Two months later, at the end of January, our Christmas decorations were still up. Andy and Mary had been the first on the block to take theirs down, on New Year's Day, and one by one the neighbors followed. Wreaths were removed from doors, illuminated plastic candy canes were plucked from snow-covered lawns, lights were pulled from rooftops and returned carefully to their boxes. But over at the Finch house garland clung to the porch posts, a wooden nutcracker cheerfully greeted visitors at the door with all the relevance of a month-late sympathy card, and sprays of holly hung by large red bows from our garage lanterns. I hadn't gotten around to taking it all down. Or shaving, for that matter, or visiting my customers. I had finally taken Kristen's advice and was trying to shift my worldview—not to align precisely with hers, but enough to meet somewhere in the middle. If our perfect was in fact all around me, then I wanted to be able to access it. Since December, all of my mental energy had been invested in understanding how I might accomplish that.

The challenge lay in overcoming conventional logic: only perfect is perfect, so any other marital circumstances would be—by definition— imperfect. The only solution I could conceive of was to redefine *perfection*. At first that meant erasing any value I had previously assigned to the word in relation to marriage. *Constant bliss*—gone. *Traditional division of labor*—outta there. *Easy, painless, matchy-matchy*—see ya. This exercise wasn't exactly easy. The only reason I was able to shed my long-standing definitions of *perfection* was that I had absolutely no other choice. Reality was going to stick around for a while, whether I liked it or not. I realized that if I was going to appreciate the gifts of my marriage and stop coveting my neighbor's life, then redefining *perfection* would be the only path to get me there.

Taking a closer look at the meaning of *perfect* provoked a number of questions, such as *How did we end up here?* and *Wasn't our relationship indeed perfect back when we were dating?* It was easy to see that reality and my intentions diverged the moment Kristen and I said "I do." When we were dating, everything felt perfect, yes, but then again I hadn't expected Kristen to come over and do my laundry, cook all my meals, and dust underneath my bed. A girlfriend didn't do those things, per my definition. Kristen never led me to believe that she was Susie Homemaker, yet I had assumed that a wholesale shift in her priorities would come with time, marriage, and kids. Besides, I couldn't get over how lucky I was to be with her. I was not at all focused on what I thought she should be doing. I was simply focused on making myself better for her.

More interesting still were the insights about myself that resulted from a month and a half of feverish journaling. For one, I quickly realized that I had no business holding Kristen to any standard of homemaking because I had clearly failed to deliver any sense of normalcy myself. It's safe to assume that Kristen didn't spend her childhood dreaming of someday marrying a guy who would tote around a personal instruction manual reminding himself not to melt down when her family reunion goes thirty minutes longer than the invitations indicated. *Kristen is no June Cleaver,* I wrote. *But then, I'm no Ward. So if she's not June, and I'm not Ward, how can I expect us to be all Ward-and-June-Cleaver like my parents or Andy and Mary? If anything, we're like a heterosexual adaptation of* The Odd Couple. (There you have it, folks—the single most imbecilic personal breakthrough in recorded history.)

While my neighborhood was busy putting the Christmas season to rest I had finally made some progress. Andy sent me text messages asking me to keep the lights up another three weeks because he had bet money on the middle of February. *Whatever.* I didn't mind being judged by the neighborhood. If I was going to be the asshole with the gauche decorated house and the enlightened path to a joyful marriage, so be it. I wasn't trying to get laid by the neighbors.

Undefining *perfection* seemed like a supreme victory in my quest to learn how to go with the flow. But having discarded all troublesome preconceptions about marriage, I found myself eager to redefine it. I mentioned this to Kristen one evening, and as usual, she encouraged me not to try so hard. "You'll find perfection if you're not looking for it."

Later that night, Kristen suggested that we should treat ourselves to an overnight stay in Chicago without the kids. It would be our first night alone together in over three years, and before she could finish asking if I was interested, I told her to book it. The next day, we made arrangements for a babysitter; a few days after that, we were checking into our hotel with only one suitcase, which we'd packed with pajamas, a change of clothes, and a couple bottles of wine.

With the entire glowing and twinkling city at our fingertips, Kristen and I wound up under the covers in our pajamas, watching television. And it felt so . . . *perfect*. So us.

I asked Kristen what she thought Andy and Mary would be doing had they been the ones vacationing in the city that evening.

"Who cares?" she said, handing me her empty wineglass for a refill. A few minutes later, she asked, "Did you figure out what makes me perfect yet?"

"Not yet," I said. "But I know you are, somehow."

"Even though I'm totally not the homemaker you thought I'd be?"

"Yeah, even though. I'm sorry that I expected that from you, and I'm sorry that it took me so long to get here." *That* felt good to say.

"I don't blame you," Kristen said. "Heck, *I'd* love to have a wife like Mary."

Then she asked me if I knew why I was perfect for her, and I drew a blank. "Is it because you have to tell me how to function like a normal person?" I asked. *What girl doesn't love that?*

"No. It's because I know you'd do anything for me, you get me, and you make me laugh, which makes me happy."

She nestled up against me and I looked down at the tip of her cute nose hovering above my chest. I settled back and my mind wandered off to a moment earlier in the evening, when Kristen had instinctively placed her pillow on the window side of the bed because she knows I'm afraid of heights and being close to a twentieth-story window would bother me. Then I thought of all the times she was patient and guided me when I needed help, whether I knew it or not: *Just relax and enjoy this with me. Stop looking, and you'll find our version of perfect. Please come talk to me, whatever's on your mind.* I thought of all the difficult tests we'd survived and how she had never left me, how she remained loyal and supportive and willing to love me. Then I looked to our future and easily imagined us doing whatever love might call us to do for each other, no questions asked, time after time. To be for each other that one person who makes the other's life the best and brightest it could possibly be. Then Kristen burped and started laughing, and there it was: our perfect was revealing itself to me, moment by imperfect moment.

Chapter 8

Be loyal to your true stakeholders.

I *am so lost right now,* I thought, rocking backward in my chair. *Seriously. I have no idea what we're talking about.*

It was the middle of February and I had been sitting in my manager Clint's office for what seemed like an eternity. Clint was conducting my annual performance review, and I was having difficulty concentrating on what he was saying. It had been two weeks since my getaway in Chicago with Kristen—our first blissful weekend together in years—and my mind was still there, loitering in the moment.

Clint had been talking at length about something—something important, no doubt. Had he told me to pay close attention, I would have been leaning forward in my chair, taking copious notes. I would have responded with affirmative comments and asked detailed questions. I would have given serious thought to the resources and the actions necessary to accomplish whatever the hell he needed. But he never said to pay attention.

My entire life, my Asperger's/ADD/obsessive-compulsive brain has focused on whatever it wants, often at the expense of things that other people think I should focus on: critical work assignments, for example, and the needs of my wife and children. I have to be reminded to focus on things like these. Clint hadn't reminded me. When I entered his office and took my seat, he had started talking without any warning and instead of processing the point he was trying to make, I concentrated on the sound of his voice, its timbral qualities and the severely Iowan way in which he formed his vowels. This often happens, which is why I occasionally chuckle or grimace at odd times during a conversation; in the midst of some benign or somber moment the speaker might hit a word with strange emphasis, and I'll begin wondering how they stumbled upon such a hilarious pronunciation ("Last night, in line at the car *warsh,* my husband suffered a fatal heart attack." *Warsh? Ha!*). The downside of my preoccupation is that at some point the listener is bound to realize I haven't been paying attention. The upside is that my profound awareness of how people say and do things qualified me as the top impressionist in my office, a skill that came in handy whenever I needed to make people laugh—which, given the awkward situations I routinely found myself in, was almost all the time.

There was the sound of Clint's voice, and then there were the visual distractions in his office. My reflection in the window behind him, for instance. *(Hmm. This is how I look sitting in Clint's office, totally confused. I wonder if he likes the shape of my head.)* Or the picture frame on his desk, featuring a figurine of a golfer at the end of his swing. Inside the frame was a picture of Clint's wife, striking the same pose as the figurine. I'd never been able to figure out which came first—the photo or the frame. It seemed impossibly dumb luck to have found a frame that perfectly matched the picture; remove the luck, however, and the whole thing just seemed impossibly dumb—to have found a frame, then to take his wife to the driving range with a bucketful of balls, snapping picture after picture until she got it right. Then again, sitting atop my desk was a Post-it note reminding myself of a few ways to improve my marriage, so who was I to judge what other couples did?

I managed to tune into the conversation when Clint said the words "Keep up the good work." As it turned out, he had been congratulating me on surpassing all of my goals for the year. I would receive a raise in addition to my full bonus and commission, which amounted to nearly 20 percent of my salary. *Sweet,* I thought, before my mind wandered off again. Most people would find it easy to focus on something as important as their bonus and commission payout, but I wasn't too concerned. I knew that I had earned the full amount that year because, for all my quirks and focus issues, I displayed remarkable skill when it came to my job. Which was strange because my job required me to be very social, and it wasn't something I had ever intended (or wanted) to do for a living. It should have been a recipe for failure.

When I had started working for the company ten years earlier, I was a lowly laboratory engineer, fresh out of college. A lab rat. My job was to develop electronic circuits and software for our lower-tier customers. The career ladder for laboratory engineers had three rungs: lab rat, manager, and director. I was the youngest in my department by at least twenty years, and the odds of beating out a dozen other senior-level engineers to become one of two managers seemed rather small, so I never put a great deal of pressure on myself to advance. I was perfectly happy being a lab rat. My customer base consisted of audio technology companies, and while it wasn't exactly the best use of my creativity, I enjoyed playing with home theater systems and consumer audio gadgets years before they were introduced to the public. I was sometimes distracted by how cool it was to have my very own desk and my very own phone and my very own name placard outside my cubicle, and I was almost oblivious to the fact that I was working on the most cutting-edge audio technologies on the planet, but I could manage that job—it suited me. At that point I had it all—I was earning good money, I had no real responsibilities, I could order any office supply I wanted no questions asked, and my girlfriend, Kristen, was crazy about me. Life was good back then.

Four years later Kristen and I got married, and after our honeymoon I returned to work and learned that, due to a strategic reorganization in our company, my position in the laboratory had been terminated.

While my manager delivered the news, I thought about Kristen, my bride of fifteen days. I wondered how I would tell her that my job had been eliminated. I wondered what it meant about me as a husband and as a man. As a provider. A good husband, as I understood it, had a good job that paid for everything the family needed. A good husband brought home a good paycheck, and a husband without a paycheck was a failure. I didn't want to think about myself as a failure, so as my manager spoke I looked out his fourth-story window, down upon the intersection of the four- and six-lane roads that met behind our building (seven and nine, if you count turn lanes). The roads were made to accommodate massive amounts of suburban traffic during the rush periods, but at ten o'clock in the morning, they were desolate. Crossing them by foot seemed to take days; pedestrians would start walking with the signal and would find themselves sprinting the last twenty feet to make it across before the light changed. I looked down at one car sitting pathetically in a turn lane, waiting all alone for the arrow to turn from red to green, and I wondered what that driver was thinking about. Had their job just been taken away from them? Were they seeing themselves as a failure? Were they now being forced to accommodate a life change they hadn't anticipated?

My manager went on to explain that I did excellent work and that my customers spoke highly of me. In light of this, it was my position that was being terminated, not my employment. He offered me a spot on the technical marketing team.

Marketing. It was a decent-enough consolation, but I had my reservations. As a marketing engineer, I would be responsible for developing technologies that our customers would need several years down the road. I would have to pay attention to what was going on in the industry. I would have to build relationships with people, the way salesmen do. Did I mention I had my reservations?

There was also a significant cultural shift to consider. The marketing guys weren't quite as frat-boyish as the salesmen in our office, but they came pretty close. The marketing team were like party nerds—they had to be social enough to schmooze customers and technical enough to converse with engineers. Because they all reported to the most aggressive manager on the planet—a man who was, in my estimation, the human equivalent of a startled grizzly bear—they had to be aggressive, too. The marketing guys were forever barging into the lab and telling us engineers what to do, brandishing their PDAs and strong-arming us into whipping up a prototype circuit or banging out some code. Or worse, they'd nail us with the adult version of a wedgie: "I need you on a conference call in two minutes, Finch. The customer is *really* pissed off, so be prepared."

The thought of working as a marketing guy day in and day out wasn't a pleasant one, but it was a better option than quitting and trying to find a new job. So I accepted the position and was shoved rather unceremoniously into my new career. Little did I know what an ironic impact this move would have on my marriage.

As a marketing guy I was surrounded by highly, almost comically motivated people who seemed to think about only one thing: business. Win the business. Track the business. Get down to business. They also talked about achieving their goals in rather violent terms: Crush your goals. Destroy your goals. Punch your goals in the face. It was a far cry from the laboratory, where people spoke admiringly of their oscilloscopes and generally kept to themselves.

The only marketing guy who didn't seem interested in steamrollering everyone in his path was Clint. He was not yet a manager when I joined the group, but he took time to show me the ropes. Clint taught me useful business strategies, took me golfing with his customers to show me how to entertain clients, and advised me whenever I was about to jeopardize my own career by doing something incredibly stupid. Because we spent so much time together at work, people often referred to Clint as my work wife, a term to which I never really cottoned. But looking back, I suppose that's what he was. Clint was my very supportive, very homely work wife.

Even with Clint's support, I worried how I might survive in my new role with the company. I was nothing like a marketing guy. I wasn't interested in business or sales or annihilating superficial goals handed to me by someone else. Funny how the challenge of becoming a marketing guy was not unlike the challenge of being a better husband: because I wasn't particularly qualified to do it, success would require an outrageous amount of work. I wasn't born with the resources that would have naturally made me a marketing guy or a great husband, but I dove headfirst into the responsibilities of each role, albeit at different points in my life.

Not only did I have to become a marketing guy, I felt I had to become a very successful marketing guy because I was now married. The bigger the paycheck, the greater the financial security, the better the husband and father. Such a simple formula. What could possibly go wrong?

To become a marketing guy, I did what had always worked for me: I observed the people around me, studied their behaviors, and used the knowledge to create a character that would allow me to blend in. Business-Man, Kristen and I now call him. An amalgam of the most successful people I worked with, Business-Man was smooth-talking (assuming he scripted his ideas before sharing them with people). He was gregarious, wonderfully charismatic around the office, and beloved by my customers. He could always get a meeting with high-level audiences, and he knew how to take business away from competitors. He received promotions and bigger customers every year. Business-Man, in case you hadn't heard, was a pretty big deal. He was going places. His blinking Bluetooth headset, his signature "Hey there!" and his shiny new golf clubs were all the proof you'd ever need.

Business-Man was a fantastic character, and the process I employed to keep him alive—to keep my career alive and my family well funded—was something like Method acting. I became the role I was playing. No one enjoys spending time around Method actors when they're on a job, and there's a reason for that: Method actors aren't themselves when they're working, they're characters. It's annoying. I wasn't Husband anymore. I wasn't Kristen's beloved Dave anymore. I was Business-Man.

On more than one occasion, Kristen had told me, "Your job is changing you. You're not that guy, Dave. You're totally unhappy and you're bringing that home with you every day, and it's making things harder for us." She frequently urged me to quit, to find something else that would suit me better. I knew she was right, but I just couldn't see myself walking away from the security of my job, as wrong for me as the job was. In an economy where companies are laying off employees by the thousands, how does one supplant a six-figure income?

"We can change our lifestyle if we have to," Kristen told me. "I just want to have *you* back."

I couldn't see it her way. I knew that I wasn't any fun to be around— the constant arguments at home were evidence enough. I suspected my job wasn't the only cause of our problems, but I didn't yet know about my Asperger's. So I felt that if I couldn't give Kristen and the kids the great husband and father I should have been, at least I could give them financial security. After all, I had the rest of my life to master the role of family man.

"I'll just keep the job I have for now," I told Kristen. For years.

My performance review had been going pretty well, as usual. Or so I thought. Clint was done talking about my bonus and commission and was now discussing something or other while he rubbed his shin with a pencil, eraser-side down. *Weird.*

"You're not listening, are you?" he asked.

Crap. "No."

Clint laughed, but he didn't stop with the pencil. "Focus, idiot," he said. "I'm trying to tell you that you're reaching a point in your career where it would make sense to start thinking about a management path."

"Ah, yes." I nodded, trying to envision the character I'd have to assume to pull off looking like a manager. Middle-Manager Guy, perhaps, his superpower being extraordinary weight gain around the waist, ass, and chin, or the ability to select suitable wines at fancy customer dinners. No—the ability to miss my kids' soccer games without a thought.

Clint continued. "And if I'm going to groom you for management, then you need to start looking like someone who could lead a team or a department. Understand?"

I did understand. While I operated at a high level and blew away my objectives year after year, I was anything but a model employee. Most of my coworkers were at work by eight o'clock, but I didn't show up until much, much later. (It didn't matter that I often worked late into the evening, Clint just wanted me there earlier.) Little things distracted me—grave concern about the food selection for an upcoming lunch meeting, for example, or tight pants. If I couldn't concentrate, many times I would get in my car and leave. Sometimes I returned to the office after driving around for a while and collecting myself, and other times I simply went home.

I certainly wouldn't have been awarded Employee of the Month for my travel habits, either. Travel was a requirement for my job, and I couldn't stand it. The preparation, the unusual surroundings, the hotels. And worst of all, the airports. I couldn't think of anything worse than flying on a commercial airline. At airports I automatically presume that everyone inside the terminal has some disgusting infectious disease and is mentally unstable, and thanks to how my brain works, this notion becomes as real and solid as concrete. I don't *suspect* I'm right, I *know* I'm right. As a consequence, I ratchet myself into a panic that starts a few days before my trip and doesn't end until after my return flight has landed. (I tried taking Xanax once, but all that did was loosen me up enough to ask the person seated next to me if she was a terrorist.)

Over the years, I found ways to avoid flying—a point that Clint was now raising in my performance review: "As a manager, you're going to have to get comfortable traveling by plane."

The previous year, I had decided that I would no longer fly to any customer that I could drive to in eight hours or less. Using negotiation skills that Clint had personally taught me over the years, I lobbied to transfer the customers outside of my four-hundred-mile radius to colleagues in other regions, which meant I could spend more time at companies that weren't so far away. I thought it was a great idea, but Clint objected, saying that I was an idiot and that he didn't want me to spend business hours driving. I compromised, offering to limit my travel to late in the day. He rolled his eyes and finally agreed. I'd leave around four o'clock for my trips and sometimes wouldn't arrive at my destination until after midnight, but at least I didn't have to fly. Heck, I'd have taken a mule.

I wasn't always able to get out of flying. I was scheduled to go to Louisville in a few weeks, an easy seven-hour drive, but Clint was joining me on the trip, and he insisted we fly together. This posed another problem: no car rental company on the planet will guarantee you a specific make and model of rental car. My preference is the Toyota Camry. I don't drive one myself, but I know that of all the vehicles offered by rental companies, the Toyota Camry has the best reputation for reliability. So, Toyota Camry it is.

Before my performance review began, I had spent a few hours trying to get one of the car rental desks in Louisville's Standiford airport to commit to holding a Toyota Camry for me:

149

"All we can guarantee is the car type—standard, midsize, or full," the clerk said. "We cannot promise you a Toyota Camry."

"But the trip is two weeks from now and that should give you time to hold one," I said.

"I can't do that, sir. I'm sorry."

I adjusted my posture. "I don't think I'm making my point clearly enough. I have to drive a Toyota Camry. I need to know if you can hold one for me."

"Sir, again, we cannot promise to hold a Toyota Camry. Why not request one at the rental counter when you arrive?"

I tightened my grip on the handset. "How many Toyota Camrys do you have in your fleet at Standiford?"

"Our *fleet*? I'm not sure I know what you mean."

"I mean, how many Toyota Camrys do you have available on any given day? Five Toyota Camrys? Ten?" The clerk sighed and I heard a flurry of keystrokes on his keyboard.

"Why do you need a Camry?"

I don't know, asshole, why do you breathe air? Would you like it if breathing air was this difficult for you? I didn't want to be troublesome; he was only following policy, and frankly, I didn't want to deal with my craziness any more than he did. But there we were. I looked up at my computer monitor, hoping that it might have a convincing answer flashing across it, something to conclude the argument in my favor. I was so frustrated that I wanted to cry. *This doesn't need to be so hard.*

"I don't know what to tell you," I said. "I just prefer to drive a Toyota Camry. I know how they steer, I know where the mirror adjustment thing is, I just . . . I need a Toyota Camry." My heart was beating heavily, and I repeated myself. "I need a Toyota Camry."

"Sir, I do apologize. If you'd like me to go ahead and make a reservation we will do the best we can to—"

"Okay. Please, make the reservation. And note that I want a Toyota Camry, goddammit."

I slammed the phone down and my ear tuned into the familiar, stomach-knotting chuckles of the sales guy sitting in the cubicle across from me. "You okay, Finchy?" he asked. He didn't know that I had Asperger syndrome; he just thought I was a freak. He drove a Toyota Avalon—a Camry for rich people. *Fuck him.*

This was how it went with every car rental counter at Standiford that morning, and this was what would go down every time I needed to travel for work. By lunchtime, I had four car reservations set for the date of our arrival: Hertz, Avis, Enterprise, and Thrifty. This was the sort of thing Clint was referring to when he said he needed me to look more managerial. More "normal."

Sadly, even with all these idiosyncrasies, I was still a much better employee than I was a husband or father. One doesn't set out to be a top performer at work by driving his marriage into the ground, necessarily. At least I didn't. But then, the relationship between an employee and his managers and customers is vastly different from that of a husband and father to his wife and children. My business relationships—my managers, coworkers, and customers—didn't require a great deal of connection or empathy. The connections I made with these people were superficial, everybody knew it, and we were all fine with it. Managers, for instance, don't need a buddy, they need an employee. They define clear objectives and provide explicit direction. There is nothing to infer, only goals to achieve. Because I stopped at nothing to achieve goals, managers appreciated me.

There is also very little guesswork when it comes to a customer's needs. There is some maneuvering and strategy involved in convincing them to agree to a sales pitch, but once they're interested in whatever it is you're selling, they spell out their needs in no uncertain terms: "If you want to sell me a microprocessor, here are the features I need. This is the quantity I need, this is the price I want, this is when I need them, this is the type of support I'm going to require." I would jot it all down in my notebook, making it impossible not to deliver exactly what they

151

needed. Detailed contracts were signed. It was all black-and-white, no guesswork, *impossible* to screw up.

My experience at home was decidedly different. There were no contracts dictating our actions; nothing was black-and-white. Empathy was a requirement. When Kristen, Emily, and Parker needed something, they didn't want to have to explain it to me. They didn't want to define clear objectives for me and provide explicit direction for how I needed to support them. They needed me to understand them like a normal husband and father would. They needed me to participate in our relationships, but I couldn't.

I never felt particularly proud of my accomplishments at work, probably because on some level I was aware of my shortcomings as a family man. In the time since I had returned from my honeymoon, my job title had gone up several notches. I had become responsible for driving the technology strategies for a handful of large customers. Sitting on my bookshelf were half a dozen corporate-recognition plaques lauding my performance and dedication to the company. But what had I accomplished at home in those five years? I had alienated my wife, my best friend. I had lost her admiration. I had fathered two children but I hadn't exactly participated in the process of raising them. If I had performed like that at work, I'd have been fired. Yet Kristen still supported me, still loved me. She never left me. And my kids were constantly giving me another chance: "Daddy's home! Can we play, Daddy?" How had they not earned my loyalty? My dedication? My full participation?

At work, we were constantly being lectured on the concept of disruptive innovation: breaking the status quo and improving your business by introducing new ideas, new technologies, new ways of doing things. With my Journal of Best Practices, I had disrupted five stagnant years of marital status quo. The result? I was finally starting to question what was really important to me. I was on a mission to define my true priorities. I was examining myself rather carefully, and sometimes quite literally—staring at my reflection in the window behind Clint's desk, for instance, as he rambled on about my career path—and I wasn't always proud of what I was seeing.

My performance review was almost over, and I was starting to get antsy. I wanted to go back to my desk and make my hotel reservation for our trip to Louisville, and I knew I had to call the hotel before four o'clock because that was when I was most likely to speak with Jennifer, the only person at the front desk who willingly broke her back accommodating my requests. ("Okay, Mr. Finch, we have you all set for one night, arriving on the nineteenth . . . I've indicated that you will be arriving in a Toyota Camry, which, again, makes no difference to us . . . Got you a standard room, king-size bed, nonsmoking, foam pillows, two wake-up calls, and we'll put you as far away from other guests as possible. Will you be needing anything else, Mr. Finch?")

Clint leaned back in his chair. "Let's review your stakeholder map," he said. "Put it up."

Ah, the stakeholder map. Of course. "Ta-da," I said, securing a piece of paper to Clint's wall with some rather expensive pushpins I'd ordered for the occasion. (You gotta love office supplies.) "Feast your eyes on *that,* bitch."

Laughing, Clint waved me off. "Move, idiot, I can't see it. Nice pushpins."

If I had any lingering doubt about who in my life deserved the very best from me, this tedious exercise was about to eliminate it. A frantic-looking spreadsheet arranged by customer name, in descending order of their commercial (read: personal) worth, the stakeholder map clearly defined on whom I needed to focus my time and energy. It captured the key people in my career who could help me to grow my business. The people who would use me, and the people whom I would use. The stakeholders. This map, we had been told by a department head, was the *single most important tool of a successful businessman.* (Prior to the stakeholder map, we had learned the *single most important tool of a successful businessman* was a well-defined strategy, and the month before that, the *single most important tool* was some sort of pyramid-shaped thing that I never fully understood.)

The stakeholder map included customers' names, titles, strategic programs to which they were linked, and the status of my relationships with them, measured as *Adversarial, Poor, Neutral, Good,* or *Proponent.* A column for general notes about the customer was also included, which I used for such comments as *Three kids—two in college; wife's name is Deborah; laughs too hard at racial humor.* Most of the guys in my department left that column empty. Actually, looking back, most of them didn't even bother to complete a stakeholder map, and those who did certainly didn't hang it above their desks as we'd all been instructed to do. But I did. With outrageously expensive pushpins, no less—Business-Man was such an overachiever.

Most of the relationships on my map had been marked as either *Good* or *Proponent.* To me, this was a clear and depressing reminder of how I had defined my priorities in life. I brought my A-game for the people on that list because I had to—if I didn't deliver for them, my career would suffer. Unlike my wife and children, my professional stakeholders only got to see me at my best—they only knew Business-Man. I stayed up nights preparing technology presentations for those people. I traveled to places like Louisville for those people. I sat alone in my hotel room, taping Kleenex to anything I might have to touch—the remote control, the doorknob, the light switches—while they ate dinner at home with their families.

Clint, however, was over the moon about my stakeholder map: "Dave, this looks great. You're really making inroads at these accounts." He was about to review the map one stakeholder at a time when his cell phone rang and he excused himself. As he exited, he didn't say, "Let's take a break," or "Meet me back here in a few." He said, "Hang on."

So I waited.

Forty-five minutes later, Clint had yet to return. *Okay, this is insane.* I peeked outside his office door and saw no one, so I walked over to his computer, curious to read the comments he was putting in my performance review. (This was unprofessional on my part, but then I was certain I could have leveraged a case for abusive treatment once I hit the forty-minute mark.) In a section titled "Performance Factors," Clint had been asked to indicate areas in which I'd exhibited significant strengths, as well as any areas needing development. There were only two areas in which he felt I needed development—organization (probably because he'd ridden in my car) and working more closely with third parties—but he had indicated six major strengths. The first three were creativity, achievement of objectives, and quality of work. No surprises there. The next three strengths—adaptability, communication, and autonomy—seemed a bit ironic. I scrolled down and saw my overall score: Very Good. By definition, this score meant that I had "exceeded objectives in several areas and required only occasional supervision."

I didn't appreciate the real irony of Clint's assessment until I looked at my stakeholder map and considered how I might have scored had Kristen conducted a similar evaluation at home. What score would I have received for adaptability? The review form defined this as "being open to change with new circumstances." *Going with the flow.* We had just begun to work on my openness to change at home, and I was still learning how to adjust to this new mind-set. Meanwhile, at work, I presented myself as nothing if not adaptable. "Sure, I'll take a new position on the marketing team." "Of course I can stay until midnight tonight. Whatever it takes." "Certainly, Clint, I'll travel to customers every week. Anything else?" At home, Kristen asked me to help fold laundry and my head almost exploded. I guessed that I would receive Needs Development for that one.

How about autonomy and initiative? Clint seemed to think that I was bursting with it, but Kristen would have offered a different opinion. "Initiative? Please. How is me having to remind you to turn off the television and play with the kids initiative? I'll put you down for a Needs Development," I imagined her saying.

Achievement of objectives would have gotten me a high mark with Kristen, until I scrolled down farther and read the definition, which included the phrase "gets things done efficiently and in a timely manner." I thought of the Christmas decorations drooping from our eaves. I thought of the countless times Kristen and I had been late for an engagement and she'd found me standing in my boxers in front of the mirror making faces.

I started feeling overwhelmingly disappointed in myself, but then I read the definition of "quality of work," on which I knew Kristen would have scored me as highly as possible: "employee strives to do the right things right and seeks continuous improvement." There was hope. I thought about what Kristen and I were accomplishing with my Journal of Best Practices. I realized that if I had successfully redefined something as huge as my version of an ideal marriage, then I could certainly redefine my priorities with respect to work and family life. My greatest contribution to my family wouldn't have to be financial if I shifted my priorities. I could actually focus on being a worthy husband and father—not developing a character to play the part, but becoming the real thing—and I could let my professional life accommodate that.

I looked at my stakeholder map, at the rows upon rows of people who couldn't care less about me, who just needed a warm body who would cater to their needs—the people who got my best hours every week. The people who always got to see me smile and hear me laugh. The people who had come to rely on me to make their lives easier. And I had one thought: *Fuck you people. No offense.*

I was in a much better mood when Clint finally returned to his office, although I was more anxious than ever to get home.

"Dude, are you still in here?" he asked, looking surprised.

"Well, yeah! You said to wait."

"Idiot, that was like an hour ago!" He erupted in hysterical laughter. "What the hell's the matter with you? Dave, next time I tell you to hang on, if it's longer than five minutes, just leave!" He caught his breath and asked me again what was wrong with me.

"I didn't want to be insubordinate." *I should probably tell him that I have Asperger syndrome and I take commands literally, but nah. Nobody needs to know.*

We proceeded with the remainder of my review. I couldn't pay attention, of course, but I didn't really have to. I'd read the scores on my evaluation. I understood that the tone of our meeting was congratulatory. I understood what I needed to do, and finally, I understood who my real stakeholders were. *Clint is right,* I thought. *Things are going well, but there's a lot of work yet to be done.*

Chapter 9

Take notes.

I drove home from work after my performance review thinking about my relationship with Kristen, my usual drive-time topic. I couldn't shake the spirit of personal assessment, and as a result I was evaluating our relationship through a different, more analytical lens.

It had been eleven months since my diagnosis—eleven months since I'd embarked on this quest to become a better husband. When we first started all this, I presumed that by the one-year mark I would have been cured of all my problematic Asperger's symptoms. I figured by that time Kristen and I would be the iconic happy couple doing the sorts of things that nauseate real people: eating ice cream from each other's cones, for instance, or ice-skating beneath the stars in a crowded rink surrounded by high-rises and Christmas lights. Our weekend in Chicago, perfect as it had been, had changed all that for me. I was willing to part with the romantic icons, but there was a sort of fulfillment—namely, the sort of fulfillment that might compel two people to actually *go* ice-skating or to share ice cream—that we hadn't quite achieved, and I wasn't willing to let go of it.

Kristen had gone so far as to explain why I was a perfect match for her, but once again I felt as though I hadn't yet transformed myself into the husband I wanted to be. I wasn't perfect enough. This notion sprang forth during my performance review earlier in the day and took my mind hostage. There's nothing like a corporate employee evaluation process to snuff out any feelings of romance or joie de vivre. Then again, there's nothing like an employee evaluation to help you see yourself as others see you—including the parts of you they try their hardest not to look at. Those are the things that are sometimes best left ignored, but I didn't know that. I didn't want to be perfect-ish for Kristen. I wanted to be perfect. The only question was how I might get there.

Sitting at a red light behind a sleek, black Mercedes, I finally made the connection. My company invested a great deal of time and resources into developing procedures that would ensure that all employees performed at their highest potential. Goals were established, and most important, things like project milestones and employee performance were tracked and reviewed at regular intervals. It was hard not to be successful when every step you took was measured, analyzed, and discussed. *Why not approach my personal reconstruction project with the same fervor?* I felt my eyes light up. *Brilliant!* I reached into my glove box and removed an expired vehicle registration card, and across the back of it I wrote <u>PERFORMANCE REVIEWS.</u> *Identify strengths, weaknesses. Set goals, track progress.* "This is going to be great!" I declared aloud to no one, drumming my hands excitedly against the steering wheel.

That evening, I joined Kristen in our master bathroom, eager to get her on board with my new plan. She was sitting on the edge of our bathtub doing something to the bottom of her foot with a rock. Scrubbing, it seemed.

"Need something?" she asked without looking up.

I shut the door behind me, stepped over the towel she had spread out on the floor, and parked myself against the sink.

"Today I figured out how we can change our lives for the better and I want to talk to you about it," I said, using my Business-Man voice.

"What, are you enlisting me in a pyramid scheme? You can drop the voice, by the way."

"No, this is about me becoming a better husband," I said in my normal register.

Kristen paused a moment, glancing at the bathroom door as though she were contemplating a quick exit. She sighed. "Go ahead," she said, resuming her scrubbing.

I began by telling her about my employee evaluation earlier in the day and that I couldn't help but wonder how she might have scored me as a husband had we conducted a similar evaluation at home.

"And what did you decide?" she asked.

"Well, I think I would do all right if we evaluated my performance as a husband since last March. But just all right." She didn't say anything. "That's not good enough. I want a perfect score."

Kristen set down the stone and wiped her foot with the towel.

"Dave, we've been over this. You're fine. You're a great husband. I couldn't be happier. Pass me that lotion, please. The one you're sitting on."

Handing Kristen her bottle of peppermint-plum foot lotion, I couldn't help but feel patronized. I couldn't tell if I was reading her correctly, but she seemed a tad dismissive.

"Well, thanks," I said, "but I don't think I'm a great husband yet. I'm getting better, but I want to do more."

"Okay," she said, rubbing a dab of lotion onto the bottom of her foot. "So, what does this have to do with changing our lives for the better?"

I explained that since my epiphany in Chicago, I had come to appreciate her and our marriage on a whole new level. More than ever, I wanted to be the best husband I could be, but I feared I wouldn't get there without a more formal approach to my process of Best Practices.

"I think we need to start conducting performance reviews on a regular basis," I said. "We need to be able to monitor my progress and identify areas that still need improvement."

"Performance reviews? You can't do this to yourself, Dave. Really. Things are fine."

"Fine isn't excellent. Come on. Surely there are things I still need to work on. Name a few. Let's hear it."

Finally, Kristen looked me square in the eye. "Dave, seriously, you need to stop. This is stupid." She ran the tub water to rinse her hands, as though the conversation were already over.

"It's not stupid," I said. "It's brilliant." I clearly wasn't gaining any ground. I knew Business-Man could have easily sold her on the idea of performance reviews, but apparently this wasn't the time or place for Business-Man. I was going to have to get Kristen's buy-in using my own devices. Namely, badgering. "Kristen, I mean it, let's hash this out. How am I doing on communication? What's my score? Fair? Average? Excellent?"

"Oh boy." She winced. "This ought to be fun."

"What? What's your problem?"

"You want to know what still needs work, Dave? Empathy." Kristen stood up, pointing the foot lotion at me. *Uh-oh.* "How about that, Dave? I'm trying to relax and do my thing and you march in here, telling me what a lousy person you are and how I need to hold you accountable to some ridiculous standard that you're putting on yourself. And I feel like I'm telling you every day, 'We're good. Relax. I'm happy.' But you can't let it go. And no matter what I say, you ignore it and tell me how I need to feel. I'm so sick of this."

She stood there, arms akimbo, glaring at me. I didn't know what to say. This was not the reaction I'd hoped for. All I was trying to do was to get her to sign off on my brilliant idea, and now I didn't know if I should argue back, or apologize, or what. Then, before I could figure out how to respond, Kristen took a deep breath, ran her hands through her hair, and calmly, as though she suddenly remembered that she was speaking to her husband and not her husband's syndrome, said, "I'm sorry. I didn't mean to blow up, Dave. I love your brain to pieces but it handles empathy rather differently, and I get frustrated."

"I understand." I smiled. "I'm sorry, too." Because this clearly needed to be about her for a moment, I didn't bother to mention that my lack of empathy was frustrating for me as well. But it was.

Although I now knew enough to say "I understand" in moments like these, I hadn't made a whole lot of improvement since last summer when we began working on my difficulty with empathy. For example, while I had become much better at listening, I still needed to be told *when* to listen. I continued to have difficulty inferring the true emotional meaning behind Kristen's body language and the things she said to me; I was constantly asking her to clarify her statements and emotions. All of this, as far as I was concerned, was more evidence supporting my theory that true empathy is God-given and damned hard to learn. I couldn't build up my empathy skills because I had none to start with; I felt like a weight lifter who'd been born without biceps. My Empathy Quotient was still a crummy fifteen out of eighty. Unless we figured out a way to make do, my deficiencies in empathy would continue to test our relationship. If I wanted to be the ideal partner, I knew that we would have to resolve this issue once and for all.

Kristen sat back down on the edge of the tub and stared blankly at her toes. It didn't take a mind reader to ascertain that she felt sad and annoyed. I could have apologized once again and left her alone, but that didn't feel like the right thing to do, so I kept the conversation going.

"As for empathy," I said carefully, "I can learn to tune in to your feelings, and I can learn how to be more responsive. You'll just have to tell me what you're feeling and what I need to do. At first, anyway, before it becomes second nature like all the other stuff we're working on."

Kristen closed her eyes and massaged her forehead with her fingertips.

"Like, right now," I said. "Obviously, you're thinking something. Are you still annoyed? Are you sad? What is it?"

"Nothing. Forget it."

I sat down next to her, rested my elbows on my knees, and folded my hands. But I didn't look her in the eye. Instead, like her, I stared down at her manicured toes while she wiggled them up and down. "Kristen, this is what I'm talking about. You have to help me understand what you're thinking if we're ever going to get anywhere."

"I just wish this wasn't so hard for you," she said, finally. "I just wish that you were normal. And I don't mean that the way it sounds. It's just . . ." I glanced up at her reflection in the mirror and saw that she was trying not to cry.

"Go ahead," I said, folding my arms. "Say what you need to say."

"Me telling you what I'm feeling every five seconds and how I need you to react is not empathy."

"No, it's not. But we're not talking about empathy anymore. We're talking about what happens after empathy. We're talking about sympathy. Feeling your emotions and responding to your needs are different things. I think I can be more tuned in and responsive without this magic ability to divine whatever it is you're feeling. We'll just work on it together, like we're working on everything else."

She nodded, looking somewhere beyond the bathroom door.

"I mean, who knows? Maybe it will become second nature to me. I'll just be walking around, reading your cues, knowing what's up without having to ask. I'll be like, 'Okay, I get it. You're late for work and you can't find your other shoe. Maybe it's not the best time to share my idea for an invisibility cloak.'"

164

She kept nodding, kept staring. But now she was smiling. "Yep. That'll be you."

I sat up and wrapped my arm around her waist.

"Oh, oh, hang on," I said softly. "I think it's starting to work already. I'm empathying something."

"Oh, really?" She chuckled and blew her nose into a wadded-up tissue that she'd removed from her pocket. I thought it was gross that she had been carrying it around, but I wasn't going to say anything.

"Yeah, wait, I'm getting a reading. It's a strong one. Okay, I'm empathying that you . . . are incredibly turned on by your husband right now and you feel a strong desire to have sex with him, preferably within the next ten to twenty minutes. Am I right?"

She laughed. "*Totally* right. You're an amazingly quick study."

"Good. See? I know this will work. And I'm telling you, these performance reviews are going to be the best things for us."

Kristen rolled her eyes and chuckled again. "Okay, fine. We'll try it. What do you want me to do?"

I described my vision for how the performance reviews could be structured and the sorts of things we might accomplish. For our first one, I suggested that we focus primarily on how I could be more responsive to her needs. "That's a good place to start," she said. "Just give me a few days to get my thoughts in order."

A couple days later, we convened in the bedroom after the kids were asleep. I powered up my laptop while Kristen changed into her pajamas and washed her face. I had been preparing myself for something rather formal. Something with charts and spreadsheets and a clearly defined agenda. I had even reserved one of the laptop projectors from the office and brought it home. I was making room on top of my nightstand for it when Kristen walked out of the bathroom, pointed to it, and asked, "What's that thing for?" Then she made me take it downstairs.

When I returned she was sitting cross-legged in the middle of the bed with a spiral notebook on her lap. Our bed is very tall, and sitting there alone on the pillow-top mattress, sinking into the thick quilt, Kristen appeared to be floating on a cloud. I had intended to sit in the leather chair in the far corner of the bedroom, thinking it would lend the discussion a veneer of formality, but Kristen in her PJs made the bed too inviting. I arranged myself across from her, propped up by pillows that I'd stacked against the headboard, and rested my laptop on my legs.

"Are you sure you want to do this?" she asked.

"If you're ready to evaluate my performance and talk about ways that I can be more responsive to you, then I definitely want to listen."

"Okay. It's just a lot to drop on you all at once, and I feel bad about that, but I don't know how else to do it."

"There is no other way to do it. This is the real value of performance reviews. Trust me."

"Okay," she said. "Just know that, in general, I'm very happy and I don't mean for any of this to hurt you. I don't want you to freak out."

"I won't freak out."

"And seriously. Turn off your computer."

I did, and at her request, I listened as she spoke. I didn't challenge her comments or derail her train of thought. I just listened.

She started by discussing the things she felt were going well. More help with the housework, lots more constructive conversation and friendly, casual chitchats, which she loved so dearly. She thanked me for the littler, less critical Best Practices I'd been working on, such as coming to bed more quietly and not talking with a phony British accent so much.

Then she turned a page in her notebook. There were still a few areas of family interest that needed to improve, she said. My level of participation with the kids, for one thing. "Also, you need to learn to anticipate your own meltdowns before they happen so that you can manage them better in front of our kids, or better yet, deactivate them altogether. The kids can't see you flipping out all the time."

She turned another page, and things got serious. We had stepped into sensitive territory. Kristen began talking about times I had let her down and the pattern of selfishness and unresponsiveness she'd dealt with throughout our marriage. As she related a series of painful incidents, incidents that I would have rather not thought about, I was forced to consider her perspective on some of the darkest moments in our marriage, the worst of which being the time that I was home on Christmas vacation two years before. I had been looking forward to two weeks of R & R. But Kristen used the time that I was home to do things for herself that she never had a chance to do, getting her hair cut, getting caught up on work, and visiting with friends, while I stayed home alone with the kids. The first week was exhausting and I quickly became bitter and angry. My vacation was harder work than work was, and I was agitated by the unexpected shift in my plans. One afternoon I finally snapped and said the ugliest words I've ever said to Kristen: "This is unfair because unlike you, I can't just pack up the kids and ship them over to Mary's all week and then pretend like I've been raising them." Hearing this, Kristen looked broken. Her face, her eyes, her entire body seemed cold and lifeless as she said the only words she could muster: "Fuck you, Dave." She left the house without telling me where she was going. She returned a few hours later, and that night, standing in the kitchen with the same defeated expression, asked me, "Do you want to be in this marriage anymore? If we ended it tomorrow, would you even care?"

Kristen's voice trembled as she told me how she had felt alone and depressed in these moments. Her grip on the notebook had tightened and I saw that her handwriting on these pages was uncharacteristically frantic. Certain words had been underlined multiple times—*high maintenance*, and *TOO MUCH DRAMA!!!*

"I do not appreciate all your little comments about Mary raising our kids. Mary is not raising our children, Mary is *watching* our children. There is a difference. I am raising our children, Dave, and I happen to work. In fact, lots of moms work. It hurts me when you say shit like that, and it's not fair . . ."

She went on, and I started feeling overwhelmed. It was not only the cumulative weight of all these painful experiences but the urge to make up for them as soon as possible. I couldn't erase five years of relative neglect and misunderstanding, but I could make sure it wouldn't happen anymore. Enough was enough. But first I had to stop her.

"Kristen?"

She set her notebook down. "What?"

"I'm sorry for interrupting you. But I need to take notes."

"Go right ahead."

The Best Practices worked because I wrote them down. I worked through my thoughts on paper, and I distilled them into rules I could follow. Once an idea existed on paper it felt more tangible. I could touch it, stare at it, carry it around with me, or put it away when I needed to. It couldn't disappear as mental notes sometimes did. At work, I wrote everything down. Why wouldn't I make the same effort at home? Nothing could have been more important than what Kristen had chosen to share with me—honest emotions and insights into how my behaviors had hurt her and driven a wedge between us. We had laid the groundwork over the past eleven months, and whether she knew it or not, she was presenting me with what I'd come to know as my "advanced topics"—goals that would have been far beyond my reach a year before. Goals that would elevate our relationship to new heights. Here Kristen thought she was just venting, but because I'd chosen to listen, she was actually giving me direction.

I grabbed my journal and over the next hour, I took three pages of notes on areas where I wanted to show improvement. Three more pages to add to my Journal of Best Practices.

Of all the people I know, I'm the only one who would ever take notes during an ass-kicking. But it was the greatest thing I could have done. Taking notes allowed me to slow down the discussion, to understand her points. It also provided some emotional buffer. Rather than getting overly emotional, I could respond constructively and focus on decoding the underlying problems and solutions. It allowed me to be proactive rather than defensive. Slowing the emotions down by taking notes was the best way for me to process what she said and use it to influence real change in my behaviors.

The upside was that by the end of the evening I was holding in my hands a road map to marital happiness. The downside was that real action would be required to pull it off—none of the comments suggested I rest on my laurels or take more naps. From everything she'd told me that evening, it was clear that if we were going to move forward, then I was going to have to become a well-functioning, fully autonomous man. Or, as I discovered during our laundry fiasco a few months earlier, I was going to have to become an adult. She had been right after all; this was not going to be easy.

Kristen fell asleep not long after we finished talking. I didn't want to go to bed without a plan for turning things around once and for all, so while she slept, I analyzed my notes in an attempt to extract some kind of strategy:

> —*Respect Kristen's personal time and space.*
> —*Be more involved with the kids.*
> —*Manage yourself and your emotions—Kristen shouldn't have to do that.*
> —*Have fun while we do things rather than making everything a "drama fest."*

The single unifying concept seemed to be: *Kristen and the kids need you to be able to manage yourself by yourself.* Sitting on the bed, with

Kristen sound asleep, I once again found myself with a worthy goal and no idea how to define the first step toward achieving it. I was ready to call it a night when one of my notes leaped out at me from the page: *Help lighten her burden by showing <u>initiative</u> once in a while.*

There it was. I realized that if I could take initiative when it came to things like stabilizing my moods then Kristen would be able to go about her day without having to worry about what might set me off. With a sense of initiative, I might actually vacuum once in a while or take the kids to the grocery store so that Kristen could enjoy some downtime—downtime that would be sweetened by the fact that she didn't have to ask for it. Initiative could make me seem more empathic. *Boo-yah.*

I wrote the word *Initiative* on a scrap of paper and taped it to the bottom of my mirror in the bathroom. I would see it whenever I washed my hands, brushed my teeth, or shaved, and it would remind me of what I needed to do that day to be the husband I knew Kristen deserved.

Chapter 10

Give Kristen time to shower without crowding her.

The next morning, I woke up at seven o'clock, half an hour earlier than usual. I looked around the empty bedroom, heard the kids playing downstairs, and it occurred to me that Kristen had been downstairs with the kids for an hour and a half. *Oh, shit,* I thought. *I have a new stack of Best Practices to work on.*

With that, I headed straight for the bathroom. I meant to study the features of my face for a little while, but there, taped to the mirror, was my scrap of paper: *Initiative.*

Damn it.

After washing my hands, I shuffled over to my nightstand and pulled out my notes from the previous evening. In determined handwriting I had scrawled *Kristen needs time in the morning to shower and get ready for work.* Compared to the more advanced topics on the list, such as *Be more present in our family's moments* and *Take a break from your own head once in a while,* the shower-time thing seemed relatively easy to master. I'd start there.

Normally on workdays, Kristen would wake up at five thirty or six, a few minutes before the kids, and try to take a quick shower. Inevitably the shower would wake up Emily because her room was next to our bathroom. Emily would toddle past me, sound asleep in my bed, to join Kristen in the bathroom until she finished showering. Then they'd wake up Parker and go downstairs for breakfast. After breakfast (so I'm told) Kristen would play with the kids before returning to our bathroom to finish getting ready, while they crowded her and played at her feet. All I ever saw of this process was the tail end, when Kristen would emerge from the bathroom to kiss me good-bye and tell me she was taking the kids next door to Mary's. That's when my day would begin.

How can I make time for her to get ready without interfering with my own routine? I wondered, sitting down on the edge of our bed. *Maybe she could wake up a half hour earlier, say five A.M.?* I didn't think that would work.

Another option was to wake myself up a little earlier, shorten my own shower, and use the extra time to get the kids ready while Kristen did whatever she needed to do. But shortening my daily soak wouldn't work either. We'd tried it once, a long time ago (long before my diagnosis), after I'd taken an hour-long shower and left her with no hot water. "Are you kidding?" she'd yelled at me, shivering under the stream of chilly water. The next morning she took action, intercepting me as I meandered naked toward the bathroom.

"Okay," she said, "I don't know what you're doing in there for an hour, but today you're going to learn how to shower from head to toe in less than five minutes. I'm going to show you."

Five minutes?! "Who showers in five minutes?"

"Come on," she said. "Chop chop. Time's a-wasting." She opened the shower door and turned on the water.

"Aren't you going to take your clothes off?" I asked, reaching for her shirt.

"No, I'm going to stand out here and help you." She batted my hand away and folded her arms. "You need to learn how to do this." Disappointed, I stepped into the shower, and she shut the door behind me.

"Start washing your hair," she instructed.

"I don't start with my hair."

"Your way takes an hour. Start washing your hair."

She had me there. Kristen typically gets ready in about a tenth of the time it takes me—hair, makeup, sixteen outfit rearrangements, and she's out of there in ten minutes. I decided to go all in and follow her instructions, knowing all the while that I'd be discombobulated for the rest of the day. I must not have told her how important my shower routine was to my daily functioning. I must not have known.

She continued guiding me through what she called a "normal process": get in, wash, and get out. It was all business and nowhere near as enjoyable as my typical shower: wander in, stand with the hot water on my back for ten or twenty minutes, soak my head when the moment feels right, see which patterns and words emerge from the square tiles, write some thoughts in the steam on the shower door, recite the contents of the soap bottle and wash my torso, recite the shampoo ingredients and wash my hair, and so forth.

With Kristen's help, I completed the shower in four minutes. She was beaming.

"You did it," she said. "How does it feel?"

"That was fucking horrible," I said, scowling and drying off. "What kind of maniac showers like this every morning?"

It was the first and last time I took a shower that short.

The notes I had taken the night before were screaming at me: *Let her decide when she'll take her shower!* I grabbed my phone and texted Clint at work:

Morning looking dicey. Will probably be late.

Then I headed downstairs to see how this was all going to work out.

Kristen was setting the kids' plates down on the kitchen table, and I could see that she hadn't showered yet. Emily and Parker climbed up into their chairs, ready to eat. The box of frozen waffles lay empty on the counter next to the toaster, its inner plastic pouch resting not far away, near the sink. The soy-butter container was still open, a crumby butter knife sitting atop its rim. Little dollops of syrup dotted the countertop, and for some reason, Emily's doll was lying facedown in the sink. Normally, I would have shaken my pillow-creased head, thinking, *Can't you keep this kitchen clean in the mornings?* but I was determined to show only initiative.

"Hey, Kris," I said, "I can get this. Why don't you go upstairs and get ready for work?"

"Oh," she said, stopping in her tracks with a bottle of orange juice in her hand. She looked stunned. "Okay. Thanks!"

I blinked my eyes, and when they reopened, she was already upstairs, the bottle of orange juice practically suspended in the air where she had been standing.

I looked at Emily. She looked at me like I was a substitute teacher.

"Mommy says I can have some more orange juice," she said.

Orange juice. Orange juice. I looked at the clock: 7:36. The request was outside of my comprehension. More to the point, it was outside of my routine. Normally, I went downstairs in the morning to accomplish only the following: drink a lot of water, take my ADD medication and vitamins, eat my breakfast in front of the television, and then scurry back upstairs for my luxurious shower. Like breathing, this process was essential to my getting through the day alive. I couldn't be interrupted or bothered, or else I'd get thrown off. When that happened, I'd melt down and we'd all lose. Hadn't Kristen explained all of this to our two- and three-year-olds?

"Umm . . . okay, hang on," I said. "I'll be right back."

I shuffled back upstairs, where Kristen was getting undressed. She partially covered herself with her shirt when I opened the bedroom door.

"Nice!" I said. She rolled her eyes and I continued. "Can Emily have more orange juice?"

"Yes."

"Okay."

"Okay then." She nodded. "Anything else?"

"No. All right, have a good shower."

I shut the door behind me, wishing that Kristen would call off this whole experiment on my behalf and go back to taking care of everything.

As I poured Emily's juice, she advised me that now would be a good time to hand out their vitamins. "The orange ones, the purple ones, and the white ones," she specified.

Vitamins . . . Vitamins . . . Parker dropped his waffle on the floor and burst into tears. "Parker, it's okay, bud. Daddy will get it, just a second." *I haven't taken my meds yet. Everyone calm down.*

Emily repeated her request for vitamins, and I couldn't take it. "Sweetie, go upstairs and ask Mommy if it's okay. Daddy needs to concentrate on picking up this waffle."

"Yay!" She ran upstairs and returned a few seconds later, reporting that Mommy had okayed the vitamins.

"Oh. Umm . . . okay, hang on. I'll be right back."

I jogged back upstairs. *I'd be eating cereal right now.* Getting into the bedroom was easy enough, but at some point in the last thirty seconds, Kristen had locked the bathroom door. So I grabbed the pin that we keep above the door and jimmied the lock open. She was shampooing her hair.

"Knock knock," I said.

"Dave, seriously?"

"I'm trying to exhibit initiative."

"Well . . ." She stopped herself, finishing her response with only a sigh, a sigh that seemed to say, *You're failing.*

"Anyway, what do I give the kids for vitamins?"

"Read the bottles," she said. "It's written on the bottles. Whatever the bottle says to give to them, that's what they get."

"Okay, so a multivitamin, a D vitamin, a calcium, and a probiotic?"

"You got it."

"Okay. Have a good shower. In fact, take your time this morning. I got it under control."

She didn't say anything, so I went back downstairs to administer the vitamins. I was hoping to get my routine started without further interruptions, but it was only a matter of time before Parker started trying to tell me something. After five minutes of me not understanding what he was asking for, Emily translated for him: "He says he wants you to put chocolate milk in his orange juice."

What the . . . Is this what goes on down here in the mornings? "Parker, do you want Daddy to put some chocolate milk in your orange juice?"

He nodded, as if to say, *Duh! What have I been blabbing about this whole time?*

"Oh. Umm . . . okay, hang on. I'll be right back."

This time, even the bedroom door had been locked. The shower was no longer running, and I could hear the morning news blaring from the television so that Kristen could hear it over the roar of her hair dryer. I reached for the pin above the bedroom door, but then I stopped myself. *Initiative. Come on, man. Show her you can do this.*

I wasn't sure what to do about Parker's chocolate-milk-orange-juice, so I stood in front of the bedroom door, staring at my toes. "Kris?" I called quietly. No answer. I took a deep breath and headed back to the kitchen.

"Okay, Parker, but just a little bit."

By the time Kristen came down, I had given up on servicing demands and had turned on our kids' favorite cartoon, *Wow! Wow! Wubbzy!* They sat on the couch in a trance, while I did what I could to salvage my routine.

Kristen seemed none too appreciative of my efforts. I had been expecting her to say something like "This morning proves that we are in a fifty-fifty, full-partnership, enlightened marriage. I'm so proud of you. I love you."

What I got was "Why aren't the kids ready to go to Mary's?"

"You didn't ask me to get the kids ready," I said through a mouthful of cereal.

"I didn't know I needed to ask, Dave." She looked at the clock. Two minutes to eight. "All right, I need to leave," she said. "You'll need to get them next door."

Ah, geez, come on! Are you kidding me?! I was about to ask Kristen when I was supposed to have time to get ready, but my Best Practices rushed in to save the day: *First of all, buster, this is just a little glimpse of what Kristen goes through every morning—and wouldn't some empathy feel great right about now? Second, you'd never argue with your boss or with a customer. You would just say "Okay" and be done with it. You need to be that flexible at home, remember. Go on, now. Give it a try.*

"Okay," I said.

She thanked me, gave the kids a kiss good-bye, gathered her things, and left. It wasn't the first time I had ever gotten the kids ready in the morning, but I almost never had to fly completely solo. Kristen was usually home to help, and if she wasn't, she'd set out all their clothes and leave a note for me with detailed instructions.

But there was no note, so during Kristen's first session with a client, I sent her a barrage of texts:

> Can Emily wear her green dress?
> (No, it's ripped.)
> Can Emily wear her blue dress?
> (Yes.)

Can Parker wear the gray sweatpants?
(Yes.)
Do they need boots or are shoes ok?
(It's dry. I don't care.)
Emily wants to bring her backpack.
(No response.)
Parker won't let me change him.
(No response.)
Hello??
(No response.)

It was clear that no more texts were forthcoming, so I called her. The first time, it rang four times before going to voice mail. The second time it rang twice, meaning that she had hit "Ignore Call." Finally, my calls went straight to voice mail without ringing.

That night, we talked. It was day one on the job for me as Mr. Tuned In to the Needs of Others, and I wanted some feedback from Kristen. She was working in the family room, submitting bills to insurance companies, but I figured she could make time for a brief mini performance review.

"So, I thought this morning went pretty well," I said.

"That's good," she said, reviewing one of her forms.

"It wasn't a slam dunk, I guess. I could have used some help there toward the end. All those phone calls and texts, you know. I mean, you kinda blew me off, and I didn't really appreciate that. You know?"

Kristen looked up at me and nodded.

"Anyway," I said, "I'd like to hear your first impressions."

She pressed her lips together, leaving only a tight crease where her mouth had been, while she continued staring at me. It was as if something was causing her physical pain. For a few seconds, anyway, because suddenly her face relaxed and she smiled, almost chuckled.

"I don't know what you expect me to say," she said, setting her forms down. "I guess it depends on what you thought you were trying to accomplish this morning."

I explained that I thought I was taking care of everything so she could have time to get ready for work without rushing around. "I was trying to take initiative," I said. "That's why I didn't like getting blown off."

"Okay. And at what point did you start taking initiative?" She was asking this as if she already knew the answer, like a trial lawyer.

"When I came downstairs—"

"No." She shook her head. "That wasn't it. Running into the bathroom a hundred times to ask me what to do isn't initiative. When did you start to take initiative? When did you take control of the situation?"

I caught my reflection in the glass door of our entertainment center and took a moment to hate myself for not knowing the answer.

"Was it when you turned on the television and let the kids watch cartoons?" she asked.

"No."

"Was it when you interrupted my first kid's session with fifty calls and messages?"

"Oh. No. It was after that."

"When I blew you off?"

"Yes."

"Okay, then." She let the point swirl around in my head for a minute before she continued. "Part of me was just fed up with answering your questions," she admitted. "But I knew the only way to get you going was to cut you off. I would never just ignore you for the fun of it."

I told her that it would have been so much easier—I could have gotten to work before lunch—had she just told me exactly what to do, and she reminded me that she had no one to call when she had to figure stuff out.

"You just get in there and you do it," she said. "If you're paying attention to what they need, and you're making their needs your highest priority, then you're probably going to make the same decisions that I would make."

Just like that, we were back to empathy. She picked up her forms, tapped them a few times against her knee, and got back to work. For about twenty minutes, I stared at the faceless wooden figurines of a man and a woman holding an infant on a shelf by our television, trying to imagine myself as a spectacularly tuned-in dad. I could see myself supervising breakfast with Emily and Parker and getting them through a typical day without any help, but then I tried imagining the steps it would take to get there and saw nothing.

"I'm going to have to start journaling this thing until I figure out how to assess the needs of toddlers," I said.

Kristen punched some numbers into her calculator, nodding, if only to acknowledge that I was done speaking.

"You know what I mean?" I said.

"Dave . . ." She set her stuff on the coffee table and turned to face me. She looked like she wanted to kick me in the teeth, but then she took a deep breath and her face softened. "Look, normally I wouldn't shortcut your learning process, but I can see this dragging on for months, so I'm just going to help you now."

"That would be great," I said. "Hang on while I get my journal."

When I got back, she told me to make a list: "Put down you, me, and the kids." Next, she told me to write down what I thought each person had needed that morning. *Oh, I see where she's going with this.* I completed my list and read it back to her:

MORNING-TIME NEEDS:
Me—water, breakfast, medication, vitamins, shower, get ready
for work, orderly start to my day, give Kristen time to shower
Kris—shower, get ready for work
Kids—breakfast

Written down, it was hard not to see where my focus lay.

"Wow. So, I don't need to eat breakfast?" she asked. I added *breakfast* to my Kris line, and she continued: "And all the kids need to do is eat breakfast? Hmm. Parker doesn't need his diaper changed? They don't need some time to cuddle with us and get their engines started? They don't need help getting dressed? They don't need someone to explain to them what they're doing that day?"

"Jesus Christ," I said, shaking my head, trying to keep up.

"See what I mean?" She smiled.

"Hang on . . ." I finished writing down her comments and immediately started thinking. How was I supposed to get through my day without focusing entirely on myself? If I wasn't going to be allowed to assign the highest priority to my own needs, then who would? No one?

Suddenly, the simple task of giving Kristen time to shower seemed like the hardest thing ever. I'd spent the afternoon at work explaining space vector modulation to eggheads. That task wasn't without its challenges, but in terms of relative difficulty, it couldn't hold a candle to this particular Best Practice, a Best Practice that essentially translated to *Pay attention to your family*.

"I am a piece of shit," I said. "I'm so sorry."

"You're not a piece of shit, Dave. You're just focused inward. Meanwhile, there's a whole world that exists outside of you and sometimes you just don't see it. Not unless somebody shows you it's there or reminds you to see it. We're all out here."

"So if I'm not naturally aware of other people's needs, then we need to define a process that will help me overcome that. Right?"

Kristen looked at me blankly for a second, then explained that there was no process, that it was just a matter of engaging with people and putting my needs at a lower priority. It seemed so simple to her, as though I'd told her that my eyes were drying out and she was instructing me to blink. "In the mornings—or anytime—you just have to remember that there are other people who are trying to have a life, too."

She went on to coach me a little bit about spending time with the kids, explaining something else seemingly obvious: that I'm the adult—the dad. "So, when the kids need something, you just need to get in, work it out, and move on to the next thing. That's the initiative piece. The empathy component may come along, but only if you're present. And you can only be present if you're actively engaging with us."

Every morning for the next several weeks, I tried mastering a new routine that would allow Kristen plenty of time to get ready. Most mornings, she had at least thirty minutes to herself without interruption and I considered that a success. A half hour may sound like no great shakes, but compared to the amount of alone time I had been giving her—zero minutes—it was a considerable improvement. The end goal was being met, but there were significant problems. Without my normal morning routine, I had no idea how to get to work on time. Kristen encouraged me to multitask—to take a short shower while the kids played in our bedroom, for instance—but as someone who took sixty-minute showers, it was clear that I had a hard enough time single-tasking.

I just couldn't merge the kids into my morning routine. While their needs were every bit as urgent as mine, they seemed to operate with no sense of routine whatsoever. Parker would demand a bagel, Emily orange juice, and as I'd service one of those requests, Parker would insist that he wanted to go look inside the potty; Emily would then say that she had to *go* potty, so I'd tell Parker not to play in the bathroom until she was done, resulting in tears. *A house full of toys and you need to play with a toilet?* On her way to the bathroom, Emily would suddenly change her mind and demand a waffle and—in the same breath—ask for a change of clothes. "Is my waffle ready yet, Daddy? Can I go upstairs and pick out a dress?" *Waffle? Dress? What happened to orange juice?! My God, can we just do one thing at a time?*

My approach to managing this insanity was to let it run its course and to try to remain calm long enough to get the kids over to Mary's house. All I asked was that they give me enough time to chug a glass of water and take my medicine and vitamins. The remainder of my wake-up process could wait until they were next door.

Mary opened her doors at eight thirty, and our kids were there—messy haired and oddly dressed—on the dot. This was one of the few things I could do punctually, though it was motivated purely by self-preservation; every minute the kids were home past eight thirty was another step closer to a daddy meltdown. By eight forty, my toast would be ready. By nine, I'd be heading for the shower. Somewhere around ten or ten thirty, I'd leave for work, and the hour commute got me to my desk by eleven thirty. Just in time to log in, review my e-mails, and then go to lunch—right on schedule.

Clint called me into his office one afternoon and, in the most exasperated tone of voice I'd ever heard from him, asked me what the hell was going on.

"I mean, seriously, dude," he said, "I allow flexible hours, but this eleven thirty shit has to stop. It makes *me* look bad to my boss when he sees you rolling in so late."

"I'm sorry," I said. I didn't know how to explain that I had willfully and radically rearranged my priorities and, as a consequence, no longer gave a damn about work. Sure, I was willing to maintain my Business-Man persona, but only in ways that suited me as a family man. "I'll try to work it out so I get in sooner."

"Don't try, idiot. Do. Ten o'clock. That's the latest I want you coming in."

"Ten o'clock . . ." I shook my head and let out a long, contemplative sigh. I did the math, working backward from ten o'clock: *Leave the house by nine. Kids over to Mary's at eight thirty, which gives me only thirty minutes to eat, shower, and get dressed. That won't work. The alternative is waking up earlier, like around six. No fucking way.* "I don't know if that's going to work."

He laughed. "Ten o'clock. Make it happen."

I knew I couldn't give him a plausible explanation for my eleven thirty start time. No one in the chain of command above me at work would care about my Best Practices. So, in the end, I lied. "Ten o'clock it is."

Chapter 11

Be present in moments with the kids.

My failure to establish an efficient morning routine with the kids was frustrating, but it seemed rather insignificant once I realized the reason behind it: I was failing as a father. I was by no means an abject failure—Emily and Parker were healthy, they never lacked for any material thing, they loved me, and they loved spending time with me—but I certainly wasn't the father I wanted to be.

I didn't realize the extent of my shortcomings until after I assumed the responsibility of getting the kids ready in the mornings, and I could see, moment by moment, what a challenge it presented for me. I don't presume that managing two spirited toddlers at breakfast is easy for anyone, but for me, it went much deeper: I wasn't connecting with them at all. Some days, breakfast was the only time I got to see Emily and Parker, and—according to my brain—they weren't my kids for that hour, they were my chores.

In servicing Emily's and Parker's morning needs, I found it easiest to detach from them. I discouraged talking, and playing was out of the question. As I saw it, the task at hand was to feed them and get them out the door as quickly and painlessly as possible. By limiting my participation, morning moments became all about extinguishing fires: make the breakfast, change the diaper, interrupt the food fight. While the approach got me through an average morning without mishap, none of us were enjoying it very much. The most I could hope to extract from our mornings together, depressingly enough, was a sense of accomplishment in completing the daily exercise. That's not being a dad. That's being a babysitter. A bad one, at that.

At 8:29, my patience fried, I'd bark at them: "Come here so I can put on your shoes. Emily, put that doll down. No, you can't color a picture right now, we have to hurry. Emily, put the doll down and put on your shoes. Parker, put your pants back on. Emily, go stand by the door. Parker, sit down so I can put your shoes on. You guys aren't listening, and I swear to God I'm going to start throwing toys away if that's what it will take."

At 8:31, I'd kiss them both good-bye in Mary's entryway, telling them that I loved them. (I hadn't exactly shown the love all morning but hoped that a few words would let them know.) Parker would usually kiss me and run off to find a toy after telling me, "My muvvoo koo, Gaggy," which meant, "I love you, too, Daddy." Despite all of the barking and scolding and freaking out I'd subjected them to over the past hour in desperate attempts to keep them 100 percent under control, Emily would want me to pick her up and hold her. "Just a few more minutes, Daddy," she'd whisper. I'd pick her up, squeezing her close. She'd wrap her arms and legs around me as far as she could stretch them, and suddenly, almost cruelly, I would become present. With her hair tickling my cheek, her body light in my arms, and her feet clinging to my sides, I would realize that I had wasted a perfectly good hour of bonding. Then in a whisper she'd tell me, "I don't want you to go."

I wish I could be a better dad for you. "I don't want to go either, sweetie," I'd say over a lump in my throat. "But Daddy has to go to work now."

We'd stand in the entryway, swaying back and forth, each of us wishing that things could be different.

After a couple of minutes, Mary would usually dream up some miraculous distraction—something she knew Emily loved to do, like painting a picture or helping her make fresh bread. Emily would slide down my stomach and legs to the floor. Taking Mary's hand, she'd walk slowly, hesitantly, away.

On the short walk back to our house, my emotions would spin out of control while my mind processed a single thought: *I am not good enough for my children.* Overwhelming guilt would become crushing sadness somewhere in Mary's driveway. *I am not good enough for my children.* Sadness would turn into self-hatred somewhere in our driveway, which would soften to regret moments later. *I am not good enough for my children.* I would carry that regret around until I got home at the end of the day; that's when the kids would bombard me, tripping over themselves to give me hugs and ask me to play with them—a moment perfect for erasing guilt, perfect for redemption—only to hear me say that I just needed a few minutes alone to settle in first. "We'll play later, okay?"

Kristen and I had been married almost two years when she became pregnant with Emily. What should have been the most joyful and exciting time of our life became, for me, something new to worry about. *Hooray, we're having a baby! Wait, wait. What about our house? We can't raise our baby in a town house—the walls are too thin. We're going to need to build a new house for our baby. Our baby! Oh, shit, I don't know how to be a dad! Dads are supposed to keep their cars clean! Dads are supposed to read the newspaper and know what's going on in the world! Dads are supposed to know how to interact with children!*

David Finch

Yet my car was a mess, like a teenager's. I had never once read a newspaper, although it wasn't for lack of trying—in my handful of attempts, I'd gotten distracted by the texture of the paper. The last thought—*Dads are supposed to know how to interact with children!*—troubled me the most. At that point in our lives, my experiences with young children hadn't been the greatest. Once when I was a teenager I fell asleep—stone-cold asleep—while babysitting an eighteen-month-old for some friends of my parents. I woke up when they returned home; the air in the family room was thick with the singular scent of fully loaded diaper. Contrary to my parents' assessment, being exceptionally good at math does not a babysitter make. Lesson learned. I also had a few younger cousins—very sweet kids—who would have been fun to play with had I any idea what to do with them. Technically I was the closest to them in age, which qualified me as someone who should have known how to play with them. I didn't. *Maybe they'd like to roughhouse,* I'd think, lowering myself to the floor and encouraging them to stomp on my face until supper was ready.

My record as an adult wasn't so good, either. I had been told that my first niece, who had just begun to walk, "love-love-loved" being surprised. "Stand behind the wall by the stairs," my brother told me. "When she comes around the corner, jump out and surprise her. It's the cutest thing." It seemed everyone else had a comparatively tame interpretation of the phrase "jump out and surprise her." Thirty seconds later, Kristen, my brother, and my sister-in-law watched in horror as my niece rounded the corner and I pounced, screaming at the top of my lungs and fluttering my hands in her face. She didn't seem to love-love-love it.

Despite the fact that I couldn't handle spending time around anyone else's youngsters, I always wanted kids of my own. I didn't understand what that really meant, of course. I doubt if anyone does. Like almost anything real life has to offer, I assumed parenthood amounted to the stuff I saw happening in sitcoms and movies—two young parents swoon over their cooing infant; years later they're skipping through a zoo holding hands as a family; invaluable life lessons are imparted moments before the limo arrives on prom night; flash forward to the eldest child returning home from college abroad, a little surprise visit to the graying parents who still have time and energy for a quick game of horse in the driveway, just like old times.

Before we became parents, I had myself pegged as a regular *Cosby Show*–certified family man—wise, good-humored, nothing if not perfectly qualified to raise children. Discipline would come naturally, and I'd know how to tie knots. Family moments would be something to treasure, rich, no doubt, with a spirit of joy and affection. Nothing would be more fulfilling than . . . oh hell, I didn't know . . . doing whatever it was people did with kids.

Three years into fatherhood, my time with Emily and Parker had begun to feel empty. I loved them, but I wasn't loving time spent with them. I understood that I was supposed to react to key defining moments in their development—lying with Parker for the first time in his new big-kid bed, Emily's first preschool recital. I understood the significance of those moments, and I recorded them in my memory. But I didn't feel as much as I thought I should.

I hadn't always felt so disconnected. I knew how to spend time with Emily and Parker when they were babies; with babies, it's impossible not to feel precisely whatever the moment creates. I felt satisfied holding them or plopping down with them on a blanket in the soft grass, their sweetly scented heads protected from the sun by oversized bonnets. I loved tickling their irresistible, round tummies and watching them figure out how to lift their heads up, how to roll themselves over, how to crawl, and finally, how to stand up and walk.

But standing on their own, Emily and Parker became individuals. They started forming opinions. They learned how to engage with us, how to ask for things they couldn't have and how to refuse things they needed. They started inventing their own games with confusing, insane rules ("Daddy, you hold this crown. Parker, you go inside the refrigerator and hand me food. When I say 'stop,' we all clap, and the first one who hops the longest wins the biggest fork ever"). They even started creating their own versions of familiar games, oblivious to the traditional rules. We would play hide-and-seek, for instance, and as soon as I'd count to ten and begin my search, Emily would leap out from behind a wall and tag me, declaring me "it," while Parker would call from the other room, "I'm in the playhouse!" When I'd try explaining the rules for the umpteenth time, they would become antsy and suggest a new game to play, at which point I'd get annoyed and find some reason to excuse myself. "I'd better go fold that laundry now. You kids play."

Kristen sometimes watched from the sidelines, confounded by my inability to participate. She told me that I seemed checked-out, that I was missing too much. During our performance review, she told me that as the kids got older, the opportunities to spend time with them would change and diminish. "We'll never have this period of their lives back, Dave. For your own sake, I wish you could engage with them and get something out of it."

While I knew what parenthood was supposed to look like, I didn't know what I was supposed to extract from the time spent with our kids. Should I be seeking a sense of pride in educating them, or a sense of decency in raising them to value discipline and courtesy, or what? I discussed this one day with Kristen, and she responded, "They're only this age once. Yes, we need to teach them things, and yes, we need to keep them disciplined. But if you're wondering what it is you should be extracting from your moments with them, it's joy. Period."

I began looking for the joy and was disappointed—a little troubled, actually—when I couldn't find it. What I did find was that Kristen's assessment had been perfectly accurate: I may have occupied the same space as Emily and Parker, but I wasn't present. My mind was often somewhere else when I was with them, so I started following where it went. Sometimes, I was preoccupied with whatever we were playing, wondering how I could make it better or more efficient. I wasn't thinking about making the *experience* better, just analyzing the circumstances: *This tower of blocks would be more sturdy if we used a wider base and cantilevered those upper terraces. We'll have to reconstruct it, and maybe when we do, I can use the colors to teach them about groups and patterns. I should videotape this. But first I need to get a blanket to sit on, this floor is so hard.*

Most often I was thinking about other things I could have been doing, such as mowing the lawn or relaxing in front of the television. Kristen would sometimes have to remind me that I was supposed to be playing.

"Parker has been asking you over and over to help him rebuild his tower. Don't you hear him?"

I would admit that, no, I hadn't heard him, that I had drifted away to my own little world, and then I'd log it in my journal: *When building towers, figuring out the best and worst things to say to pregnant women can wait. Pay attention!*

Understanding where my focus went was helpful, but I didn't know what to do next, so I asked Kristen to help me flesh out a strategy for more meaningful involvement. She didn't feel that was necessary. "There's no trick to enjoying your time with the kids, Dave. It's not a process. Just be present. I don't know how else to say it."

I wrote her advice down on a Post-it note—*Be present in moments with the kids*—and stuck it to our kitchen counter. I had written those words maybe a dozen times since our performance review and still they hadn't sunk in. All I could think was, *How?* I couldn't ask Kristen to explain it. How would a neurotypical go about explaining something as elemental as engaging with the outside world? It would be like me telling her, "Go solve some differential equations." Her brain just doesn't work that way.

I spent weeks trying to force myself to be present with nothing to show for it. Then one day in the spring, I was outside on our patio watching Emily and Parker hunt for worms in our flower beds in their old Halloween costumes. Emily was a cow and Parker a lobster—surf 'n' turf. They would find a fat night crawler and take turns holding it and squealing with delight before running to the swing set to give the worm a ride. After about a minute, on Emily's command, Parker would turn the worm loose and they'd run back to the flower beds to find another one.

It was a beautiful, quiet day. The daffodils that lined the curved seating wall of our patio were in bloom, and the flowering dogwoods we had planted the previous year were starting to fill out, their leaves lending a soft voice to the breeze. I closed my eyes and took a deep breath, and it finally hit me: *If you want to be present, just be present. You can't force it. You can't overthink it.* Insisting on being present, in and of itself, detaches a person from a moment. By making a conscious effort to engage and connect, you end up thinking rather than feeling, and you miss the moment completely. Nothing numbs feelings like thoughts.

Unfortunately, I tend to be more analytical. My exceptional need for control and order often defeats my ability to be present and to feel. Feelings, like children, are disconnected from order and reason. Although feelings (like children) may have their own sort of logic, they tend to go wherever they want. But unlike children, there's no control over feelings; there's only chaos. Chaos begets uncertainty, and there is nothing scarier to someone with Asperger's than uncertainty. Logic, on the other hand, brings the world under control, and routine—sweet, sweet routine—keeps it there. That's why I rely so heavily on logical thinking and rigid routines. Lining up the items on my desktop; working Monday through Friday without exception; executing my morning regimen without interruption. These rituals create order; they pacify my mind. No surprises, no behavioral triggers, no meltdowns.

Because I tend to overthink everything, it's rather easy for me to isolate myself from a moment. That's me in the orchestra hall, unfolding my copy of the score and following along, measure by measure, while the music swells and the people around me dab their tears dry. That's me during the Fourth of July fireworks trying to identify trajectory patterns in the expanding bubbles of sparks while the other spectators gasp about whatever it is they find so moving. It may have been what Kristen was trying to tell me all along, but experiencing joy—with children or with anything—requires one to feel. In order to feel, one must suspend analysis and critical thinking. Routine might also go out the window and—as I wrote in my Journal of Best Practices—you have to learn to allow that to happen. You have to learn to hand yourself over to the moment.

When I was a kid, being present was much easier. I don't remember resorting to logic and analysis as a child. Maybe that's because everything was already under control—my parents took care of that, so I was free to experience things as I pleased. I really didn't have anything to think about, and yet there was a lot I didn't understand. I didn't know why I loved the smell of my dad's work shirts. It didn't occur to me to consider why I could fall asleep on my mom's feet while she folded laundry. I didn't have any theories to help explain why I could stand for what seemed like an eternity in one spot in my dad's pasture, staring at the tall grass as it swayed back and forth in the sunlight or moved like waves across the hillside when the breeze picked up. In my childhood world, the grass was shiny, the sun was warm, and everything around me could be transformed into a medieval kingdom on a moment's notice.

Now I have my own kids, I thought, watching Parker try to tickle a long night crawler he'd plucked from the flower bed. *This is their childhood. It's happening right now, whether I'm present or not. They just want me to be in it.* I had finally reached a turning point.

I made a conscious decision to start surrendering myself to Emily and Parker's childhood at every available opportunity. In doing so, I found that there was some procedure to it after all—something I'm certain that even Kristen did, but she wasn't aware of it because it came naturally to her. The procedure involved two steps. First, I had to constantly remind myself to participate in their childhood whenever I was with them—whether we were at home, buying vegetables at the farmer's market, or running errands in the car. Second, I had to ask myself every time we did things together, *What is this moment* really *about? Is it about building the perfect tower of blocks? Is it about making a peanut butter and jelly sandwich without leaving a mess all over the counter? No, it's about enjoying the experience with them, so do that.*

I must say, it worked out beautifully.

"Okay," I said, trying on a pair of swimming goggles. "I think I'm ready."

It was a sunny Saturday morning in June. For three months I had been working on giving Kristen more time to herself in the mornings. I'd realized that the secret to doing so successfully was to learn how to engage with the kids, and by Mother's Day, I'd learned what engaging with them really meant. Now Father's Day was around the corner and I was standing in our upstairs hallway in my swimming trunks, watching Kristen gather towels and dry clothes for me and the kids.

"Looks like you're all set," she said, giving my waistband a little tug. "I'll send up the kids if you want to start running the water."

"You got it." I gave her a thumbs-up and headed into the bathroom.

I had offered to administer baths to the kids after breakfast ("You kids are in luck, because Daddy is giving you baths today!"), but Kristen was reluctant to let me.

"It always ends with you getting pissed off, or someone crying or going to time-out, and I just don't feel like dealing with that today," she said. "I'll just do it."

Her comment was still ringing in my head when I turned on the tub faucet and watched the water cascade into a shallow pool around the open drain. I couldn't remember the last time I had given the kids a bath, but I knew exactly what Kristen was talking about. I have a sensory issue with water. I don't mind being immersed in it or showering in it, but when water splashes me unexpectedly, I go insane. There's the surprise of the sensation—unsolicited wetness—and the uncertainty of the next hit: when it will land, where it will land. I've always had an issue with this. When I was young, we went to the beach a few times each summer and I loved it—especially swimming. But then other kids would start splashing and I'd scramble out of the water to sit by my mom under a towel until it was time to go home.

I stuck my hand under the faucet. The water was warm—just right—so I pushed the stopper down and began filling the tub. The rush of the water was so loud that I could no longer hear what was going on outside of the bathroom. My entire world had been reduced to that bath for the time being—just like when I was a kid.

If you're doing it right, giving babies and toddlers a bath is nothing but splashing. You might have a few minutes right at the beginning when they're simply mesmerized by the rushing and rising of the water. But then you have to dump water from a cup all over them and scrub them with soap, an activity that is sure to get you wet. Wet clothes are also a problem—I can't stand being in them. The sensation of damp cloth clinging to my skin sets my nerves on fire and I can't function. I become temperamental and impatient. Because of this, bath time with the kids had always been a tremendous challenge. (Despite the fact that every parenting book on the planet says that bath time is one of the best times for a dad to bond with his children.) A ten-minute bath would result in a half hour of tears from our inconsolable children after I'd removed them from the tub for behaviors that I'd deemed unacceptable, such as splashing or standing up. Our crying children would be Kristen's to deal with. This was what she had meant whenever she told me that when I was around I made things harder on everyone.

"Can't you just fucking relax and enjoy things with us?" she'd ask as I'd storm away to our bedroom to towel off and put on dry clothes. "Next time, do me a favor and don't help."

But that all changed with my backyard epiphany. I hadn't stopped hating the splashing, but I'd found a solution: the bathing suit and goggles. But those were just the price of admission to the real party, which started the moment the kids came rushing into the bathroom, completely naked, tackling me and showering me with laughter and hugs.

The bath was going rather well. My slippery kids were laughing at each other and sharing toys, and I wasn't exhausted by a sense of rage or regret. Instead, I felt fulfilled.

While Emily fashioned a hat out of bubbles, Parker examined his belly button; I couldn't help but laugh. They had finally pulled me into their world—the kingdom of childhood—and it felt profoundly familiar. The world in which I tend to isolate myself, my painful, lonely, hyper-controlled world, isn't without its charms. But as comforting as my routines are, I've never had one look at me with soap bubbles on its nose and tell me that it loves me.

Kristen came into the bathroom and kissed the top of my head. "I'm going to take a shower while the kids finish their bath," she said.

"That sounds nice," I said. "Take your time."

Just like that.

Chapter 12

Parties are supposed to be fun.

Kristen and I always have a lot to celebrate at the end of June. First there's Father's Day, followed by our wedding anniversary and my birthday. But prior to the Best Practices this two-week season of parties didn't inspire much of a celebratory mood. It always felt strange celebrating Father's Day, given that my parenting skills had been something of a disappointment for the first three years, and the tears that Kristen had shed on our third wedding anniversary spoke rather poignantly to the fact that our marriage hadn't been much to celebrate, either. That left my birthday, a day that was all about toasting the birth of the very person who had made Kristen's life miserable. But after fifteen months of hard work and soul-searching, Kristen and I were finally able to look forward to this season with real anticipation. We were communicating again, and I was beginning to hit my stride as a father and as a husband. I was folding laundry, Kristen was taking her first uninterrupted showers in years, and when *America's Next Top Model* wasn't on during its regularly scheduled hour, I stayed cool as a cucumber. And that gave us plenty of reason to break out the streamers and party hats. Heck, we could have made a layer cake.

In light of all this, I decided that June would be the best time to embark on my most ambitious Best Practice yet: being fun. A few months earlier, during the at-home performance review in which I forced Kristen to participate, she had cited a general absence of fun in our marriage as a major disappointment. "The fun is just . . . *gone*," she said, "which is confusing because before we were married, all we had was fun. I thought I married this totally social guy, and then I discovered that's not you at all, and then I felt duped."

She was right, of course. She had been duped, though not intentionally. She had fallen in love with the best version of me that I could muster—that charming, fun-loving, sociable character that I truly thought I could sustain. I was now determined to bring him back, to reintroduce the fun in our marriage. Because we'd come so far in our journey, this goal felt like extra credit, and unlike with my calculus exam in high school, I didn't intend to leave valuable points on the table. I decided to focus my efforts on being fun at parties initially, for two reasons. First, Kristen needed me to be fun in general, but especially at parties, where the only point in showing up is to have fun. Second, it was June. Party season.

In reality, I've never been one to extract any measure of fun from a party, and that's why this Best Practice seemed the most ambitious. When I was very young, for example, and my mom would have kids over to our farm to celebrate my birthday, I thought it was strange and wondered when they would ever go home so that I could finally just play with my toys by myself, the way I liked to. Even at the age of five, I was critical of the behaviors of other kids; watching them tear around our backyard, which was where I liked to sit peacefully with my Tonka trucks and compare blades of grass, gave me the feeling that everything on the farm was running amok. Generally, I liked the other kids; I just didn't care to have them on my turf—even if I got some cool presents out of it.

Besides the usual birthday parties and family events, I avoided parties until I got to college. Once there, I fell in with a group of nerdy musicians whose "parties" were something I could manage: sing a few songs a cappella toward the beginning of the party while our voices were fresh, then debate the significance of composers like John Cage until someone got so drunk or homesick that they started to cry. That was my posse; that was how we rolled.

I went to college in Miami and never once made it to South Beach. South Beach seemed to be for the population who didn't tuck their Rush concert T-shirts deep down into their pants, so I figured it was best to avoid it. South Beach was for clubbing. The few times I was invited to go with people, I declined and was branded antisocial. It didn't seem fair, considering how clubbing is, by its very nature, the single most antisocial activity imaginable. How much interacting and relationship-building can people accomplish standing waist-deep in foam and screaming at each other over Lil Jon?

"I LOVE THIS SONG!"

"WHAT? THE MUSIC IS SO LOUD! I CAN'T HEAR YOU!"

"HOW ABOUT THAT CHICK?"

"WHAT?"

"THAT CHICK OVER THERE!"

"WOW, THEY'RE DOING MAGIC OVER THERE?! HOW UNEXPECTED!"

But that's clubbing. At least you can stand for hours without saying a word in a club or sneak out without being noticed. But you can't do that at a party. At a party, you have to be present. At a party, you have to engage. Mingle. This is where my game falls apart. The social situation at a party falls way outside of my normal daily parameters. Things are not on my terms; events unfold by the terms of the gathering itself. In the midst of this, I feel that all eyes are on me—my own included—monitoring and judging my performance from start to finish. *Don't do anything wrong or unusual, because everyone will think the worst of you for the rest of your life*. It's pretty fucked-up in my opinion.

One thing that I find challenging about a gathering is the disruption to my schedule, my routine. If it's at someone else's house, we're doomed, because that's not where I usually am at four P.M. on a Saturday. I'm not familiar with their silverware, their hand towels, the sights and sounds of their home. Maybe they make their stuffing differently, or I'll be forced to sit on a couch where I have to turn my head to watch their TV, which looks and sounds different from my TV, and whatever sporting event or TBS movie marathon they're watching on mute might not be worth the stiff neck. If it's a family event, at least it's not terrible form to flip the channels. Even then, if the family member lives more than an hour away, their newscasters look different, their weather radars show a different part of the state, their local car dealership commercials are jarringly low-budget, and it all messes me up.

If Kristen and I hold a party at our house, then I'm really screwed. My whole environment is disrupted. Guests tend to hog all the good seats. They make the rooms look different, sound different, feel different. On the day of the party, our refrigerator is crowded with large, sealed bowls and dishes filled with prepared foods that I'm not allowed to touch until the guests arrive. And I don't know what to do with myself between the moment in which we finish our frantic cleaning and the moment the doorbell rings, so I pace by the front door for hours, wringing my sweaty hands and spying out the front windows to see if they're here yet. I can't do anything else. I'm anxious to open the door; invite them in with a well-rehearsed, cordial greeting; and then follow them, inevitably, to the kitchen, where I'll wait on the periphery of their small talk, looking for the perfect opportunity to escape to a dark, empty room upstairs.

There's only so much relating I can handle. Usually after six minutes, I've had enough. I have to get home, to my own thoughts, to my own TV shows on my own couch. That's where Kristen and I differ. She thrives on interaction. She derives energy from parties and talking to strangers about their recent trip to Vietnam or what it's like to be an accountant. For all she knew, I was the same way. For all she knew, I wasn't the sort of person who would shut down at parties, who would insist that visits be limited to one hour, who would cling to her side during a function, demanding that we leave.

As I geared myself up to approach this Best Practice in the months that followed our performance review, I couldn't help but think that at one time having fun with Kristen had seemed natural and effortless. We had fun together before my misguided persona ever entered the picture (dressed as he was in a toga and beer helmet). I recalled hanging out as friends. Back then, Kristen stirred everything inside of me, and because I made her laugh, made her feel like talking for hours, made her feel good about herself, I was on her mind a lot, too. We didn't need any particular reason or occasion to get together and have fun.

I'd call Kristen on a Saturday morning, "I'm going to Ikea, K-Pants. Wanna come?"

"That sounds fun. I'll pick you up in half an hour."

It was as easy as that. Any subsequent discussion about the day's plans would be mostly for the sake of staying on the phone with each other a little longer. Later, browsing the chaotic furniture displays at Ikea, we would decide we were hungry and have lunch together. We'd follow that up with a two thirty matinee and grab coffee afterward.

Back then I did everything I could think of to get her to invite me places. I probably could have chilled out and let her come to me—a tip that showed up a few times in *Cosmo*—but that wasn't really my style. When I like somebody, I'd rather latch on like a crab and not let go. "Oh, you're going to the ob-gyn? What's the address? Maybe I'll swing by and we can people-watch."

My natural personality suited our friendship just fine. But then we started dating and I began psyching myself out, thinking that now she was mine to impress or to offend, to grow old with or to lose. My friend was now my girlfriend. *I'm Kristen's boyfriend.* Every day felt like an audition. The mantra that I repeated over and over was challenging, if not paralyzing: *I'm Kristen's boyfriend, and Kristen's boyfriend must be perfect.* Perfectly dressed. Perfectly groomed. Perfectly behaved. Perfectly fun.

I was, of course, doomed. The house of cards I'd built as a sociable person could never bear the weight of real life. Before we became an item, I had been successful in disguising my social incapacities partially because I could accept or decline any invitation that came my way. Kristen celebrating the first week at her new job? I'm there. My company's Labor Day picnic? No chance. Fourth of July at Grant Park in Chicago? Please, shoot me in the face. I could go out with my friends and leave after precisely one hour, or sooner if everyone was talking about sports. But when you're the boyfriend of an amazing woman, you say yes to the Labor Day picnics, you say yes to the throngs of people in Grant Park, and you don't tell her that you need to leave a party precisely one hour after you arrive. *I must be perfect,* I thought. *Regardless of whether that's fair to either of us.*

After we fell in love I threw caution to the wind and began navigating uncharted social territory ("Sure, I'd like to attend a hippie baby shower. Tell me, will I have to eat the food?"). But I figured that I could force myself to enjoy parties as long as Kristen was there. After all, regardless of where I was, if Kristen was there, I was good. She made me feel so included, so present in social situations. So . . . not lonely. Standing next to her, I would be introduced to everyone in the room, one at a time. She would invite me to share funny stories. She would merge me rather gracefully into other people's conversations. "Oh, you're into jazz? Dave and I were just talking about his favorite drummer . . ." I was no longer that weird guy skulking around behind the fern; I was Kristen's boyfriend, and it was my pleasure to meet you.

By the time we were married, I had come to rely on Kristen to get me through every party and family get-together until we could finally go home, almost like a drug. When she no longer saw the fun in that, we started having problems. She grew tired of carrying every conversation for me, and without her help I would become uncomfortable and want to go home. She couldn't take the awkward moments I would create—fetching our shoes and coats as more guests arrived, for instance, or sitting by myself, refusing to socialize. We reached a point where if I went anywhere without her—even to the mall—I would feel not unlike a provincial traveler lost in a foreign city without his guide. And when we were out together, I knew she felt as though she were walking across a minefield: Something. Is going. To happen.

After six years, it was enough already. I wanted to be better than that, for her sake. I wanted her to be able to enjoy our relationship.

As luck would have it, my friend B.J. happened to be getting married at the end of June. I was happy for him, but I also couldn't get over what a perfect opportunity his wedding would be to show Kristen my commitment to bringing back the fun. Call me egocentric.

It helped that he was getting married in Charleston, South Carolina. When the wedding invitation arrived, Kristen asked her mom to keep the weekend clear to watch Emily and Parker. "Mommy's going on vacation!" she said, marking her calendar. Her message was crystal clear: Mommy needs to have fun.

Unbeknownst to Kristen—had she known what I was up to, she probably would have told me to chill out and stop obsessing—I decided to approach our vacation as an experiment with two objectives. The first was to stop making things less enjoyable, and the second was to actually make things more fun for her. It was a lot to cram into a short vacation, but like anyone with obsessive-compulsive tendencies, I tend to overpack.

Most people might have preferred to fly to Charleston, but Kristen was perfectly happy to spare me the agony and make a road trip of it.

Knowing how much they would miss us, and how much we would miss them, it was incredibly difficult to say good-bye to the kids when we left. But once we got on the road, Kristen found her vacation energy and I renewed my determination to be fun. When we reached the interstate about an hour east of home, Kristen plugged in my iPod, kicked off her shoes, and read me the menu of snacks available in our travel cooler. We belted out tunes karaoke-style as we buzzed past the Chicago skyline and started in on the snacks somewhere in Indiana. Kristen was in a great mood and my only responsibility was to keep it that way. I hadn't consciously done that in six years, so it felt both good and unfamiliar—like working out for the first time after years of putting it off. I didn't go overboard trying to be fun—the drive wasn't saturated with corny jokes and slide whistles. I just tried to keep myself from being the opposite of fun.

We stopped to eat somewhere in Indianapolis. By that point in the drive—the four-hour mark—Kristen was in an even better mood than when we left. I'd had exactly the same number of negative, anxious thoughts as I would have had in any four-hour period, but I had chosen not to dwell on them (this was hard but so worth the trouble), and I had chosen not to voice them. I had also had the exact same number of happy thoughts, and I'd made the same number of lighthearted observations about the things happening around us that I normally would have made ("How do sneakers get wrapped around those overhead power lines? Do you think the utility crews go out and install the shoes themselves? Is there a guy radioing back to his foreman requesting a pair of size elevens?"). The difference was that I chose to dwell on those things, because positive things kept Kristen in a good mood. Reinvesting all that energy kept our conversations positive and exploratory, rather than depressing and angry sounding. It was enjoyable.

Over lunch, I thought about the fact that all of our lives cannot be spent avoiding the negative things. We had to be able to talk to each other about things that were bothering us. We had to be able to give a voice to our frustration from time to time. But not right then. Not on vacation. Not during my experiment.

It was late in the evening when we arrived in Greenville, South Carolina. Charleston was only a few hours away, but we were tired and happy and decided that Greenville would be a good place to spend the night. We had been in stride all day—not a single freak-out from me and two of the most relaxed bare feet I had seen in years resting on the dashboard above the glove box. I had remained faithful to my experiment, and I'd stumbled upon a very important discovery: Kristen is perfectly capable of having her own fun, and if I prevent myself from derailing it, then she stays happy. *Is that what she means when she tells me to stop worrying about stuff and just let it be?*

As we got ready for bed in the hotel room, I made my second discovery of the evening.

"Kristen, did you happen to pack my syringe before we left?"

"No," she said. "I thought you packed it with your stuff."

"Hmm," I said calmly, though my head was starting to stir a little bit. "That's a shame. I forgot to pack it."

Kristen stood next to me, finding herself on eggshells for the first time in almost twenty-four hours. She had every reason to feel that way. Normally, this would have become a highly dramatic situation, even though I probably didn't even need the syringe.

Three weeks before the trip, I had had my wisdom teeth removed. I would have preferred to wait until after our trip, but the pain of my impacted teeth warranted an immediate extraction. The holes were stitched up, my mouth was stuffed with gauze, and I was given very clear instructions: "Use this special syringe to flush the sockets out with water after every meal for two to three weeks to avoid any complications such as dry sockets." *Dry sockets? Good God, that sounds terrible.* I followed the instructions exactly every day for almost three weeks, until that day.

"I'm sure it will be fine, Dave," Kristen said as reassuringly as possible. "You shouldn't have any problems at this point. I think most people stop using the syringe after a couple of weeks."

"Right." *But the doctor said two to three weeks. Wait, don't tell her that.* This was exactly the sort of thing that would send me into a tailspin and more than ever, I needed to prevent it. I pretended not to care at first, but an hour later I was lying in bed, unable to sleep. I didn't even know what dry sockets were, yet they were all I could think about.

"Kristen," I whispered, waking her up. "I'm going to run out and find a Walgreens."

She mumbled something that ended with "drive careful" and went back to sleep.

I hated myself for worrying about something as stupid as a syringe on our first day of vacation, but I figured it would be best to just find one and buy it so I could get the matter off my mind. I found two twenty-four-hour pharmacies within ten minutes of our hotel, and neither had the kind of syringe I needed, so I returned to our room and tried to calm myself down. Waking Kristen up to tell her about the fruitless search would not have been uncharacteristic, but I knew a vacation was all about doing things differently. *The stores didn't have a syringe,* I thought. *Kristen can't snap her fingers and make one appear, so why wake her up and bother her with it?* I climbed into bed, curling up behind her, and as I kissed her cheek, her mouth curled into a little smile. *So worth it. Day two starts in a few hours.* I fell asleep praying, asking God to stand by me and guide me as I worked on being fun.

The next morning, I awoke with unbelievable confidence in my transformation (it certainly helped that Kristen woke up, rolled over, and held me tight for a while). By midmorning, confidence had turned into near-cockiness; I was cracking jokes and taking turns leading our conversations. It felt like friendship. As on day one, a tremendous amount of effort was required to pull this off. It didn't feel natural, but it did feel like an accomplishment that we had been talking for hours and I hadn't annoyed Kristen once.

When we arrived in Charleston, we had a little bit of time to walk around and get acquainted with the town before B.J.'s wedding began. We ate lunch and did some window shopping, and as we strolled from storefront to storefront, Kristen took my hand and held it; it tingled as if she were holding it for the first time.

The wedding ceremony was beautiful, of course—held in a timeless old church that we were convinced was haunted.

"So beautiful," Kristen whispered during the vows.

"And so spooky," I replied.

"Oh my God. Totally."

Then it was on to the reception, which was held not far away, in the decidedly not-haunted South Carolina Aquarium.

I had little time after the ceremony to regroup and prepare for the remainder of our evening, but to my own surprise, I didn't feel as though I needed to. Positive energy, I was learning, is rather sustainable. I figured that a couple glasses of wine would help, too.

I stood in line at the bar, watching from across the lobby as Kristen introduced herself to an elderly couple standing near a large fish tank. Though there were swarms of strangers milling around, and sharks swimming overhead, all I saw were Kristen's smile and her eyes and her beautiful hair. *She's here with me and having fun!* Whether she knew it or not, Kristen didn't have to worry about me melting down or begging her to leave early. She wasn't going to have to deal with me hovering behind her or clinging to her side all night, as I had made a conscious choice to be fully autonomous during the reception.

Kristen saw me and gave a little wave, and I was transported back to an evening that I had spent with her when we were first dating. Her best friends, Valerie and Meredith (who would later become our roommate), were getting together after work, and Kristen had sent me an e-mail at lunchtime saying she'd love for me to come along. *I just love the time that I get to spend with you,* she had written.

I flipped out.

Andy and I were supposed to hang out after work, but I called him and canceled. I started organizing things on my desktop: lining up the edges of the papers, straightening the telephone cord, repeatedly tapping the keys on my calculator. Because they had nothing better to do, people in other cubicles had the nerve to answer their phones and talk to one another. Such distraction, while I struggled to pull together a mental game plan for my upcoming evening. *A night out with friends. With* her *friends. Okay. No problem. Four people, three of them talking a lot. Figure we'll meet around eight thirty, maybe stay out until midnight or so . . . I should really need only about an hour's worth of stories and maybe a handful of wisecracks . . . that would be more than enough. What could I do tonight for an hour?*

I opened my lab notebook to jot down some ideas for anecdotes. Fun anecdotes, to be specific. *Spotting a guy at the gym yesterday—no good ending. Dropping my glasses in the toilet—strong stuff. Getting chased by a goose last week—good for a few minutes, will work in a pinch.*

In my mind, I envisioned the four of us sitting in a pancake restaurant. (Why pancakes? I don't know.) I imagined Valerie telling a story from their college days, her recollection furthered by my line of thoughtful questioning. Meredith and Kristen would exchange knowing glances, silently saying to each other, "Such insightful questions! This guy is the real deal." *Yeah. I can make it work. I have to make it work, there's no other way.*

Satisfied that I had enough material to be good company for her and her friends, I began writing my response to Kristen, a note that took me close to an hour to complete. The first draft included a few drawings to supplement the jokes—dumb little stick figures that I could have attached to the e-mail as JPEGs. I took a moment to read it over, trying to imagine her reactions, and though I couldn't gauge precisely how she would react, I did have the good sense to remove the jokes and drawings altogether. *I will seem like a normal guy, busy at work, if I keep this short.* The final draft read something like "That sounds great! Your friends are so much fun." Then I added, "How's your day going?" before clicking "Send" and downing a fistful of Advil.

The evening with Valerie and Meredith went perfectly well; I'd have given my performance an A+. Kristen would have, too. I was ecstatic that night. I knew that since they were Kristen's best friends, I needed to earn their approval—not unlike how a presidential candidate needs to win Iowa. No one that I know can explain why it is so important; you just have to win it to be successful. Without the approval of her friends—the Asshole Identification Council, as they were—Kristen might have begun to doubt what she saw in me, her interest in me would have evaporated, and then I would have lost my best friend *and* my girlfriend. I would have been forced to return to my pre-Kristen life, which was rather lonely.

There is a clear distinction between being alone and feeling lonely. Being alone is not so bad. Most often, I'd prefer to be alone. It's peaceful with no one around. I can enter the world of the mind—a decidedly more comfortable place to live, since I am in complete control there. I can dream, reflect, ponder, fantasize, or just replay images and sounds in a constant loop. It's my world, my way, and because no one has access to it, it can't be contaminated, altered, or ruined. It's not a lonely state, being alone. To me, being alone is quite comforting.

Feeling lonely, on the other hand, is the worst. Logic would have it that one feels the sting of loneliness the most when one is all alone, with no one around. That's the loneliness we all know so well, the loneliness that appears when we're by ourselves, wrapping its strong arm around us, providing us, at least, with some company.

But there's a different side of loneliness, one that I see very often, and it's much more sinister. Far from consoling, this side of loneliness savors every moment of our abandonment. I see this side of loneliness when I'm out with a group of people without a prayer of being able to relate to any of them. Loneliness is being the only guy in the pub who might honk like a goose at the bartender, and knowing you're that guy. Worse than not fitting in, however, is finding someone you like and annoying them. This is part of the Asperger's package—our exuberance around people we like sometimes pushes them away. Ironic.

As a result, I'm often conflicted about going out with people. Every friendly get-together feels like the evening when my performance could make or break the relationship, and the pressure freaks me out. For neurotypicals, going Out seems to involve looking forward to a great evening of sharing, gabbing, and going with the flow. They'll enjoy themselves in clothes that look good on them without fretting over their itchy collars and cuffs as they raise their glasses and lean forward into their tables. They'll talk about sports, husbands, about other times they've been Out together. In short, going Out seems to be all about being in a moment together and having a great time. It sounds horrible.

I like In. I can't screw up In. Stay in, shut in, turn in. Unlike the people whom I meet when I'm Out, I get all of my jokes. I don't have to explain to myself why a horse driving a high-speed train would be a riot. It's easier to internally recite a phrase I heard a decade ago than it is to have a conversation with someone, and sadly, it's sometimes more satisfying. Why go to a party and suffer overwhelming real-life anxiety when I can sit on the edge of my bed and imagine myself being the most happening guy in the room? "When the boat capsized," I imagine myself saying, looking out into a sea of admiring faces, "I knew that I'd be okay, but I'd never forgive myself if I didn't swim back under the bow and rescue those very frightened orphans, many of whom I'd taught to read. Who wants more champagne?"

The problem, of course, is that in real life, I'm not suave. I haven't rescued any orphans, nor have I taught any to read. I am difficult to talk to sometimes. *And you know what?* I thought, waiting in line at the bar at the South Carolina Aquarium. *Oh well. That doesn't have to mean I can't enjoy myself when I'm around people.* Socializing wasn't my strong suit, true, but I realized I could find a way to have fun and be fun at parties by contributing in my own way. My contributions wouldn't look like everyone else's, but that didn't necessarily matter. *I think I'm onto something here.*

Prior to my diagnosis, such a revelation would not have been possible. Perhaps that's what a diagnosis does: it helps you to understand that you have unique operating parameters—unique limitations and preferences. Knowing why you don't naturally fit in alleviates the shame and embarrassment. (*That's my brain, folks. Can't help it. Who wants more champagne?*) My diagnosis gave me an explanation as to why I was relatively alone in my circumstances whenever I went places, and that knowledge somehow made me feel less lonely. Best of all, I wouldn't have to use a persona anymore. I could just be me. *These people don't realize how interesting I am! I need to show them.*

Determined to keep the magic rolling, I spent a good amount of time at the reception introducing myself to people and talking with them. There were stretches of time when Kristen got pulled into other conversations, and I consciously prevented myself from clinging to her. *Let her talk. Stand here with B.J.'s coworkers as if you need nothing from her.*

She didn't have to ask me every five seconds if I was okay or if anything was bothering me. She didn't have to manage me. Instead, we were dancing! In an aquarium, no less! At one point, a stingray floated by and I said, "Oh, there's that stingray I wanted to introduce you to. Friend of the bride, total history buff." Kristen wrapped my tie around her fingers, saying, "Look at you, party animal!"

Then, through eyes tired and sparkling with champagne, she asked me a great question.

"So, are you actually having fun tonight? Or is this just an act? Are you just playing a character right now?"

"No," I told her over the music, "I'm actually having a good time. I don't want you to be married to a character, I want you to be in love with the real deal." And I meant it. I was having fun! I didn't feel lonely, and she didn't feel trapped. I wasn't worried about my performance—hadn't even given it a second thought. I told her in general terms about my epiphany in line for cocktails earlier in the evening—that I can do my own thing—but I decided not to let her in on the fact that I was hell-bent on not being clingy or depressing. Doing so would have ruined my experiment.

Admittedly, standing around in an aquarium, eating bacon-wrapped sausages and talking to complete strangers about how they all know one another, wouldn't have been my first choice. It probably never will be. But Kristen had fun, and watching her made the evening a better time than I could have imagined.

Then I thought, *Why stop at parties? Why not be fun everywhere?*

The third day of our trip presented us with some minor challenges—little tests of character to see if the daily seeding of being great company was actually starting to take root. *Bring it.*

It was pouring down rain, for starters, my wet T-shirt no less a constant reminder of that fact than the slow, percussive rhythm of rainwater crashing to the wet Berber carpet in pea-sized droplets: *bloink . . . bloink . . . bloink.* I was standing by an unoccupied reception desk in the smallest and most depressing office lobby I'd ever seen. My cheery floral-patterned swimming trunks and sandy flip-flops seemed ironic, as did my fresh suntan. Perhaps the setting was depressing because we were on vacation and I was wasting precious time standing around in a reception area, or maybe it was just because the walls were the color of a tobacco stain and there was no one—I mean no one—around to help me.

There was a silver bell on the deserted reception desk, and next to it a handwritten sign reading RING BELL FOR ASSISTANCE.

I did. No one came. Next I called out, "Hello?" No response. Thinking I must have the wrong office, I stepped outside to read the placard mounted beside the hollow, wobbly door. DENTAL SUPPLY SUITE 1A. *This is it*. I looked out into the parking lot, through the rain coming down in gray sheets, and put my hands up as if to signal to Kristen, *I don't know what the hell is going on in there*. From inside the minivan, she shook her head and raised her hands, as if to ask me, *What the hell is going on in there?*

I went back inside—wondering why in God's name I decided to have my wisdom teeth removed three weeks before a vacation—and made sure to slam the door shut. This got someone's attention, apparently, because I heard a voice, some shuffling around, and finally, a short, bearded man emerged in a Hawaiian shirt and blue jeans.

"Hi," he said with an inquisitive smile. "I'm Ed. Can I help you?" The good news was that he didn't offer to shake my hand. The bad news was that it was because he was holding a dusty surgical mask in one hand and a white plaster mold of someone's teeth and gums in the other.

"Yes," I said. "Uhh . . . My wife and I are on vacation, and I just had my wisdom teeth taken out. I'm supposed to be using a special syringe to clean the holes out after meals, and I forgot it at home."

"Oh," he said, concerned. "Where's home?"

"Illinois."

"Oh my."

"Anyway, I've been trying to find a fine-tip syringe here in town and haven't had any luck. I saw your sign out front, and I'm hoping you might have something like that."

"Oh, like a fine-tip syringe? Like, something you'd use after a tooth extraction, you mean?"

I flashed the broad, fake smile I typically reserved for business discussions, the one I'd rehearsed maybe a million times, the one I used to ingratiate myself to someone who could help me, but only if they wanted to. "Yeah, Ed. That's exactly what I mean."

He took a moment to scratch the back of his neck with the surgical mask (because, I suppose, using the teeth would have been bad form). "You know, I think I do have something. Give me a minute, I'll be right back."

He gestured toward the rumpled green sofa behind me—the one that he had clearly brought from home, or perhaps picked up on a curb somewhere along with a floor lamp, a broken microwave, and a sign reading FREE—suggesting that I take a load off.

"Fantastic!" I said, though I had no intention of sitting on Ed's personal effects, no matter how friendly he seemed. I opened the front door and gave Kristen a big thumbs-up, and she laughed and rolled her eyes.

I was there because Kristen had caught me on the phone in the hotel room earlier in the morning, trying to get ahold of my oral surgeon. I thought Kristen was showering, but when she stepped out of the bathroom to grab her contact solution, she heard me ask in a near whisper if Dr. Bressman could advise on my situation. "See, I left my syringe at home . . ."

This seemed to have triggered a number of memories for her: our Door County vacation undermined by my fixation on avoiding West Nile virus; our Cape Cod vacation severely burdened by my obsession with the property's outdoor shower; every family gathering since 2004 ruined by, well, you name it.

"I'll call back," I said, quickly hanging up. I wanted to think that I wouldn't have turned the matter into a full-blown obsession capable of ruining day three, but Kristen wasn't prepared to take any chances.

"Dave, if you're still worried about dry sockets, we'll just find a place that sells those syringes," she said.

"But I don't want to blow our vacation. I didn't want it to be your problem."

"It's not going to blow our vacation. But if we don't find one, then I want you to stop thinking about it. Deal?"

I agreed. Leaving the third pharmacy without a syringe at around ten A.M., I called the search off, and we headed for Folly Beach, which was about a half hour from our hotel in downtown Charleston.

We sat on the sand, watching people in the water splashing one another and getting stung by jellyfish, until a thunderstorm blew up, clearing everyone from the beach. Rather than heading back to the hotel, we decided to drive around for a while, and we got lost. Happily lost. "Turn down this street," Kristen said. "I want to see those houses." After dozens of random turns, we passed by this little office complex and the sign jumped out at us: DENTAL SUPPLY.

So there I was.

Twenty minutes passed with no more sign of Ed and I started going mental. Every now and then, I could hear pounding and the unsettling sound of hacksaw-against-plastic. *Did this guy mean that he'll find me a syringe . . . when he's done doing whatever he's doing with those teeth and gums? I don't have time for this!* I rang the bell, and he didn't emerge. By that point, I figured Kristen would be massaging her temples with her fingertips, just barely keeping herself together, intensely regretting the fact that she was sitting in our minivan in a flooded parking lot in a downpour, married to a syndrome. I figured that my experiment was over. I figured that we were right back at square one, that my glory had been washed away.

I opened the office door and looked out into the rain. There she was, her head swaying back and forth as she sang along with some music. She spotted me, smiled, then lifted the iPod to her mouth, as if it were a microphone. Her singing gestures became more and more elaborate until she busted up laughing, and I thought, *All is not yet lost.*

Friendly Ed finally surfaced, marching almost, as though he had solved a great mystery.

"All right, he we are," he said, handing me something that looked like a small NASA-designed turkey baster. "How's that?"

It was a hand-cobbled syringe. *Wow.* I had been expecting something a little more hermetically sealed. A little less touched by human hands. But he seemed proud and handed it to me with a smile, so I took it.

"Thank you," I said.

"Wasn't any trouble. Just had to use the tube from a larger syringe, and glue this other tip onto it, which meant I had to join them with this middle piece here. Careful you don't tip it down until the glue dries."

I asked him how much he wanted for it and he gently refused my offer to pay him. "Free of charge," he said, opening the door for me.

I thanked him again and then dashed out to the car, eager to show Kristen my custom mouth squirter.

We decided to wait out the weather over lunch in a bar on Folly Beach. The clouds overhead were wispy and full and the color of dirty snow. But our veggie wraps were phenomenal and Kristen's face was pure sunburned happiness. Beneath a high-definition television playing reruns of dirt bike races, we shared our favorite moments from the vacation, reliving them during the rain delay. She reached for my hands from across the table and said, grinning, "This is what I remember us being. This is how it used to be."

Outside, the sun broke and the clouds rolled away, so we took our drinks to go, excited to see what fun was in store for us.

The Final Best Practice

Don't make everything a Best Practice.

Three months after B.J.'s wedding, Kristen declared a moratorium on my Best Practices. The system, she told me, had gotten out of hand. Apparently, eighteen months of constant discussion about self-improvement had finally caught up with her and she couldn't take it anymore.

Kristen didn't have a problem with my sense of determination per se, but by the end of the summer it had become clear that the Journal of Best Practices was dominating our life. "It's disrupting more than helping," she told me. "It's emotionally draining."

It is? I wondered. I hadn't noticed, but then, not surprisingly, I hadn't considered things from her perspective. Perhaps it *was* draining to talk to her husband several times a day about his own behaviors and whether he was "likable enough." Maybe it *was* disruptive to be woken up at night only to be informed of my latest plan to give her more closet space—a Best Practice I had intended to refer to as *Donate all clothes not worn in twelve months,* something I was convinced would make her think I was a truly remarkable husband.

Once she pointed it out to me, I could see that the scope of the Best Practices had expanded to include rather impertinent topics. Absurd even. By the time I mastered being fun at parties, which was not long after I began working on it, Kristen and I had addressed almost all of the underlying factors that had created problems in our marriage. With those core disciplines out of the way, I turned my attention to other, less critical things—things that amounted to minor annoyances. *Don't dawdle when mowing the lawn,* for instance, was something to keep in mind if we had to go somewhere that day, but as a Best Practice it didn't warrant the same amount of effort as *Be present in moments with the kids.* But I couldn't make that distinction. I was on a roll and I didn't want to slow the pace of transformation (see "obsessive tendencies"). I wanted to improve even more, even if it meant that my nightstand drawer—that central repository of paper scraps, Post-it notes, and journals—would collapse under the weight of my ambition. That's where Kristen and I differed.

Had I kept the process to myself, it might not have been so bad, but I always insisted on her participation, even when she had other things to do. Which was all the time. As a working mom, Kristen's days were packed. If she did have a few minutes to herself in the evenings, she would want to use that time to chill out, not to project slides against the wall to review my progress on such initiatives as keeping the refrigerator more organized and staying calm in the grocery store.

As with so many other things that are plainly obvious to most people, I had to be told that annoyances were to be expected and tolerated in any relationship, and especially in a marriage. Though I may not have realized that on my own, once it was explained to me, I understood exactly what it meant. Kristen put it this way: "You hog the blankets, Dave. You take months deciding which computer to buy. The instant we all pile into the car and shut the doors, you fart. That stuff is so annoying, and *so* not a problem."

What was a problem, she explained, was beating myself up over every little thing and creating drama that nobody needed. After all, her expectation was that the Best Practices would eliminate all the drama. (Though I don't know who she thought she was dealing with.) It was okay to aggravate her, but it wasn't okay to drop what we were doing and formulate a Best Practice anytime I did, nor was it healthy to sacrifice otherwise happy moments for the sake of analyzing problems ad nauseam. It wasn't okay to allow the Best Practices—the process of healing our relationship—to interfere with our relationship. If we did, then we'd be letting Asperger's win.

"So, let me get this straight," I said. "Even if I'm not flawless and I annoy you sometimes, you can still love me and be happy?"

"Yes! Exactly, Dave! That's what love is. That's what *marriage* is. That's what we have! Isn't that great news?"

It did sound like great news. So great that I could hardly process it. Ironically, I had to write a note in my journal reminding myself not to make everything a Best Practice. I knew that I was going to have to practice it. I envisioned myself frustrating Kristen in countless ways, and I could see myself laughing it off. *Yes, I put the empty cereal box back in the pantry. Yes, she found it and now she seems irritated. No, I'm not on trial; no, she's not keeping score. It really is no problem, just like she said, so let it go.*

What I couldn't have envisioned, however, was how much trust would be involved in allowing myself to let things go. It wasn't easy. I assumed that, like me, Kristen made judgments against everything she saw and held grudges for decades. Although she had never given me any reason to feel this way, I had always assumed that if I was anything less than flawless, she would one day pack up her things and move on to greener pastures, perhaps finding herself a no-maintenance guy who loved grilling out with the neighbors and folding clothes. Being secure in who I am was going to take some getting used to.

I'd spend the next several months mastering the skill of being loved and accepted by Kristen. I had to remind myself numerous times every day that she wasn't judging me, that she just wanted me to live my life without overthinking it. I made a pretty big deal about not making a big deal of things. The result? I no longer felt the grip of anxiety or the overwhelming sense that I was doing everything wrong. For the first time in almost ten years, I felt comfortable just going about my days. I felt reborn. Which was not a bad outcome, considering that a year and a half earlier, when our marriage was suffocating, I felt as though the entire burden of reconstruction was on my shoulders.

But a burden isn't a bad thing. My desire to become a better husband and to earn back Kristen's friendship helped us to achieve one of our primary objectives: I learned how to manage my behaviors and moods on my own. Kristen never set out to make me flawless, she just wanted me to be able to manage myself, and now I am able to do that.

That's not to say that I don't have to be careful. Far from it. Like anyone battling an affliction—be it addiction, hyperactivity, an eating disorder—I have to manage my behaviors every day if I want to be successful. If I don't, I can find myself retreating behind old habits. I forget to go with the flow, I lose sight of other people's perspectives, or I begin to absent myself from my family. Brooding, silence, resentment—it's all there, waiting for me. Even in our second year of Best Practices, I made these mistakes, usually because I became distracted by either an unexpected argument or some random short-term fixation, like lifting weights or taking nature walks. I'll probably continue to slip from time to time. My brain wouldn't have it any other way. But now when I slip, I don't fall. I know how to keep myself up, and I know how to move on. Even if I were to fall, Kristen would be right there to help me up. Laughing, the way she does when I slip and fall on my ass, both literally and figuratively. That's what marriage amounts to.

Enough about me, though. The morning the Best Practices were born (Pi Day, my fellow nerds), Kristen and I embarked on a mission with one objective in mind: to save our marriage. A worthy goal, if totally ambiguous. *Save the Earth* comes to mind: *Oh yes, definitely. Which part?* We didn't know it, but the first year and a half of saving our marriage was really about understanding who we are, what our relationship *actually* is, and what we both need to do to make it work. Eighteen months, dozens of Best Practices, and innumerable hours of soul-searching later, Kristen and I finally reached this awareness. (I'm rather amazed we lasted five years without it.)

But we still weren't there. Our marriage was better, no question, but it wasn't exactly working. When Kristen curled up next to me in bed during our weekend in Chicago and told me, "You get me," she was wrong. Or at least, wrong-ish. I didn't get her, entirely. I understood who she was, how she behaved, what made her laugh. But I didn't understand what she needed. For our marriage to work, I had to understand that.

With the final evolution of the process—*Don't make everything a Best Practice*—after two years of lugging around notebooks, folding the frigging laundry, calling for performance reviews, and interviewing myself in the shower, I finally *got* Kristen. I understood what she needed from me: put the notebook down, love her, love the kids, and simply *be*—be myself so that she can love me back. That's it. It seems unspeakably easy to me now, but perhaps I should consider that a testament to how far we have come since renewing our commitment to each other and to our relationship.

It's a funny thing. By liberating myself from the process of becoming a better husband, I actually became a better husband. I also became a better dad. But I wasn't the only one transformed by our journey; Kristen had also changed. I just had to get out of my own head long enough to notice it. Once I set my notebook aside, I saw that we had become our own perfect version of the family I'd always envisioned. In every room of our house, framed pictures now adorn the walls and tabletops, telling stories of some of our happiest moments together as a family. Granted, these pictures were all taken by other people who had framed them and given them to us as gifts, but the pictures were still of us, and we had finally managed to hang them on the walls—that's something to be proud of. We were eating homemade dinners together, dinners that Kristen had prepared while I ran through the sprinkler in the backyard with the kids, wearing my goggles and dreaming of the day when I'd be able to afford a wet suit. Kristen and I were going on dates (or rather, going on the exact same date time after time, God bless her heart). And best of all, it was *our* affectionate hugs that were now being interrupted by two little sponges squeezing in to absorb all of the love. All this from a journey to earn back my wife's friendship.

One final thought. For those of you in a relationship blessed by perfect compatibility, continual bliss, and matching clothes (I'm looking at you, Andy and Mary), I'm happy for you. Thank you for reading this book to each other under a warm blanket. For the rest of us (I'm looking at you, everyone else), when you find yourself staring defeatedly at your spouse over breakfast or watching them hunt through the dryer for a pair of socks, and you wonder, *Who in the hell did I marry?*—and you will—I can now say with absolute certainty: there is hope. You can turn things around.

I have the nightstand drawer to prove it.

Acknowledgments

Ihave been blessed with the support of many extraordinary people. I'd like to thank my parents, Jim and Mary, for a lifetime of love and encouragement. I'm also grateful to my brother, John, and his wife, Jen, for remaining in my corner, and to my wife's parents, Jim and Sandi, for loving me and accepting me as their own. My kiddos, Emily and Parker, cheered the loudest for me and colored pictures to buoy my spirits on the days when all I managed to eke out was a chapter title. Thanks to my friends B.J., Laurel, Courtney, Traci, Delemont One, Delemont Two, Greg, Jen, Phill, Meredith, Valerie, Cliff, and the best neighbors I could ask for, Andy and Mary, for their continual reassurance and clearly questionable standards of friendship.

I was fortunate to have persuaded a number of people who are much smarter than me to read my manuscript in one form or another, and their insights and perspectives made rewriting *The Journal of Best Practices* thousands of times a true joy. Many thanks to Rebecca Connelly, Laurie Cunningham, Dr. Sheila Flaherty, Justin Jones, Adina Kabaker, Kelly Kennoy, Cathy Postilion, Sylvie Sadarnac, Jason Sarna, Cathy Scherer, Michael Tirrell, the incomparable Nancy Beckett, who expertly demystified the art and process of storytelling, and the late Mary Scruggs, who urged me to write this book and left much too soon. Very special thanks to Dr. Gail Richard for her invaluable elucidation of empathy and its impact on communication and socialization, and to Dr. Simon Baron-Cohen, whose research has afforded me the luxury of understanding myself better.

Daniel Jones at the *New York Times* helped to shape the essay that became the basis for this book. Daniel has the astounding ability to express more in two sentences than I can say in two pages—had he written my acknowledgments, you'd be done reading them by now. Thank you, Daniel.

Beth Wareham welcomed me to Scribner, an opportunity for which I cannot thank her enough. I owe an overwhelming debt of gratitude to Susan Moldow, Kate Lloyd, and everyone at Scribner— thank you, thank you, thank you for your support, your enthusiasm, and all of your hard work.

Two people made a profound impact on my life recently and I'd like to thank them now. The first is my agent, Suzanne Gluck, who is one of the nicest people I know. Her extraordinary vision and unfailing support, her wisdom and guidance—these are gifts that have changed my life, and for that I'll always be grateful. The other is Samantha Martin, my tireless and strikingly intelligent editor at Scribner, who never failed to provide me with a brilliant window into my own personal journey, and who always pushed me to do better. Suzanne and Samantha, all I can say is thank you.

Most of all, I owe thanks to my wife, Kristen, who made all of this happen. This book captures only an infinitesimal sliver of everything she puts up with in a typical day, of her capacity for grace, understanding, and love. The greatest thing a man can do for himself is to marry someone who is infinitely better than he is. And that's exactly what I did. With Kristen's support, I know I can accomplish anything.

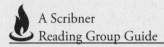

The Journal of Best Practices
David Finch

Introduction

Filled with humor and surprising insight, *The Journal of Best Practices* is David Finch's personal and candid exploration of his quest to become a better husband—in spite of and aided by his Asperger syndrome. Faced with the failings of his marriage, David embarks on a ruthless self-improvement plan full of note-taking, spousal performance reviews, and a running journal of the ways in which he can be a better partner, a better father, and a better man. A unique and moving look into life on the autism spectrum, David's is a story that shows it's never too late to change, and that love—with the right amount of hard work—can conquer all.

Topics & Questions for Discussion

1. "I was thirty years old and had been married five years when I learned that I have Asperger syndrome, a relatively mild form of autism." Discuss this opening scene in which Kristen asks David a series of questions from an Asperger's evaluation test. How does this passage establish their relationship?

2. Discuss the way David stayed on his "best behavior" in the beginning stages of his relationship with Kristen. Have you ever hid a certain personal preference, quirk, or eccentricity when first meeting someone?

Did you ever feel comfortable enough to share this part of yourself? What was the reaction?

3. David lists the four distinguishing characteristics of Asperger syndrome as "persistent, intense preoccupations; unusual rituals and behaviors; impaired social-reasoning abilities; and clinical-strength egocentricity." In what ways does he embody these characteristics? To what extent has he learned to manage them by the memoir's end?

4. Why are David's "optimized personalities" so effective for business but fall short when he is at home with his family?

5. What constitutes a lack of empathy? How does David more successfully empathize with Kristen after starting his journal?

6. List and track David's display of adaptability, or "going with the flow," over the course of the memoir—from sharing living space with Delemont and Meredith to his weekend at the wedding in Charleston.

7. Do you think there is a general set of rules for maintaining a healthy relationship? In your response consider David's admiration of Andy and Mary's marriage, his notions of being a "flawless" husband, and his redefinition of the word *perfect*.

8. How would you describe David's portrayal of Kristen in *The Journal of Best Practices*? How does she change over the course of the narrative? How would this account of their marriage differ if it were told from her perspective?

9. Did you think David's application of employee performance reviews was a good idea? Would you perform such an experiment in your own relationship?

10. When writing about his tendency to overthink things and his desire to be more present for his children, David states: "In order to feel, one must suspend analysis and critical thinking. . . . You have to learn to

hand yourself over to the moment." Do you agree? Is the key to joy the exclusion of thought?

11. Why are routines so important to us? What are some of your own daily routines? Discuss David's struggle with breaking rituals and consider how committed you are to your own.

12. Do you know anyone with an autism spectrum condition? How has your knowledge of autism spectrum conditions changed after reading *The Journal of Best Practices*?

13. Discuss David's narrative voice. Was there a particular scene or description that stands out to you? What parts made you laugh?

14. Consider David's moments of revelation, such as when he was watching *SportsCenter* and had the epiphany of "going with the flow." Why were these specific analogies helpful to David? Did you see the logic in the way they related to his condition?

15. Do you think keeping a Journal of Best Practices would be useful for a "neurotypical"? Can you apply any of David's Best Practices to your own life?

16. What inspired you or your book club to read *The Journal of Best Practices*? What are your overall thoughts about the book? What are you eager to discuss with your book club?

Enhance Your Book Club

1. Try keeping your own Journal of Best Practices and document the ways in which you interact with others. Does writing down and being aware of how you communicate and react to others benefit your relationships? What are some of the Best Practices you discovered? Discuss what it was like to keep a journal, and share your Best Practices with your book club members.

2. Discuss the epigraph by Arthur Adamov: "The only thing to know is how to use your neuroses." Reflect on your own personality. How can you channel your own neuroses or less-than-desirable personality traits for good?

3. If you're brave enough, engage in a performance review with a spouse, significant other, family member, or even with one of your book club members. How do you score? Is it easy to be honest with those closest to you?

4. Consider reading Abby Sher's *Amen Amen Amen: Memoir of a Girl Who Couldn't Stop Praying (Among Other Things)* or any book by A. J. Jacobs for your next book club selection. How do the memoirs compare? How similar are the authors' approaches to self-improvement and realization?

5. Visit www.davidfinchwriter.com to watch interviews between David and Kristen, to read the He Said and She Said blog posts, and to request David to call in to your book club discussion. Or check him out on Facebook: www.facebook.com/davidfinchwriter.

A Conversation with David and Kristen Finch

Author David Finch and his wife, Kristen, sat down with some fans at Simon & Schuster's offices in New York to discuss The Journal of Best Practices. *Here is an excerpt of that conversation.*

Q: *David seems almost comically committed to self-improvement. Was this process about fixing him?*

K: No, it was never about fixing him. Our relationship needed work, so that's what we set out to fix. Although, it's not inaccurate to say he was almost comically committed to self-improvement. Dave sometimes takes things to what many people would consider to be an extreme.

D: After we learned I have Asperger's, my first thought was that if I could simply rid myself of the condition, then I'd be someone Kristen could love. But Kristen helped me to see that I wasn't broken, that we had simply gained new insight into how I work. Still, I knew that we live in a neurotypical world—that I was married to someone from a different planet—and I was motivated to understand how I could function better in that world. Kristen was my very willing guide to her neurotypical world, and I was her guide to Aspergerland.

Q: *So fixing your marriage wasn't about overcoming Asperger's?*

D: No. I learned how to manage some of the deficits and leverage the strengths attendant with the condition—applying my hyper-focus to restoring our friendship and learning methods for going with the flow, for example—and that helped our relationship. But most of the things I needed to work on were things that every husband and wife have to work on: helping around the house, communicating, not putting empty milk cartons back in the fridge.

Q: *What Best Practice offered the biggest breakthrough?*

D: The biggest breakthrough is so hard to pin down; they were all so essential. I'd say going with the flow and tuning in to the world around me were high up there. Learning how to go with the flow and appreciating reality was what opened the door to a whole new world of joy and happiness for us. Our marriage is messy and chaotic and imperfect, and yet, it's so perfect for us.

K: Those were huge, and I think using words was a biggie. Communication enables every other aspect of the relationship, and without it we would have remained stuck.

Q: *Have all the Best Practices taken hold?*

D: Absolu—

K: NO!

D: What?!

K: Oh, come on. Laundry?!

D: I do laundry all the—

K: Let me stop you right there. I want it to be known that the laundry chapter is completely fraudulent.

D: But—

K: Nope. Fraud. Take it out, take out the whole chapter. Just yesterday I found you in there digging through the dryer for your cape, and don't try to deny it. I have pictures.

D: Ehh . . . okay, some of the Best Practices did not stick.

Q: *What's this about a cape?*

D: Let's move on.

Q: *Kristen, how did you not know that David had Asperger's?*

D: Because I'm dripping with normalcy.

K: That, and I never understood how challenging things were for you. Until we took the quiz, you'd never explained how much effort went into things I tend to take for granted, like socializing or just getting through a typical day with your sanity intact. Also, I wasn't observing you through a diagnostic lens; I was just coming home from work and spending time with my husband. Slowly the condition revealed itself to us, one confusing situation at a time.

D: Yeah. The threshold of wackiness and drama and resentment tends to creep up on you when you're married and it's just one misunderstanding after another. Things heat slowly to a boil when you're not communicating.

Q: *David describes how playing characters has served him well throughout his life. Are there still moments when you see those characters?*

K: Yes, I still see roles being played in social situations that require him to be "on." I think it helps him to navigate interactions. Businessman made an appearance recently in Boston. We were trying to get seated in a crowded restaurant, and I saw Dave go from Happy Dave to Ruthless Businessman in a split second.

Q: *Businessman showed up and took control? What happened?*

K: We were seated right away; everyone else had to wait.

D: I remember that. I had the lobster.

Q: *The characteristics you've described sound a lot like my husband. Is it possible he's on the spectrum?*

D: Sure, it's possible, but I can't speak to whether it's likely. Everybody has their quirks. Whether a person fits within the parameters of the disorder, however, depends on the degree to which certain characteristics affect his or her life.

Q: *I have another friend on the spectrum who wants nothing to do with a diagnosis. Can you offer any suggestions?*

D: You have to ask yourself, Who would benefit from this diagnosis? If you feel your friend could see how a diagnosis would help to improve his life, then perhaps you should bring it up. If, on the other hand, a diagnosis or mention of a neurological condition would further strain your relationship without leading to positive change, then perhaps it's enough that you are aware of how your friend's brain is wired. The knowledge can help you to understand who they are, and there's real value in that.

K: It's hard. The success of any relationship depends on both parties working together.

Q: *Kristen, what were some of the things you worked on?*

K: I just made a happy marriage my priority. I tried to find the balance between my go-with-the-flow nature and Dave's need for order and predictability. Our days are more structured now than they used to be. I also choose my battles—I know what Dave's triggers are and what his limits are. I know that he is more egocentric than a lot of people, but I also know it's not by choice and that he is more willing to work on being empathetic than a lot of people. That goes a long way.

D: I admire you.

K: Shut up.